Withering to Flourishing

Nine Ways to Bloom Again
After the Storm Has Passed

Cher Knebel

Visit us at www.livinghappilyconnected.com

ISBN: 978-0-578-65721-9

DEDICATION

This book is dedicated to my loving and beautiful friend Sue, who passed away from cancer and went to Heaven in January 2011. Her spirit was like a lovely garden—sunny, natural, inspiring, and simply delightful. I miss you my friend, but you are my angel now. I felt your presence throughout the entire writing of this book.

TABLE OF CONTENTS

INTRODUCTION

Where there is no struggle, there is no strength

---Oprah Winfrey

My story and how I got stuck in the muck

Before I talk about the nine things that I did to help me to start blooming again, let me share with you some of my background and how I ended up in a bad place. I have a degree in Communications and have been a professional writer for more than 30 years, working 20 of those years in corporate communications. I'm also a wife of nearly 25 years and a mother of two amazing adult daughters. I'm also a self-help-reading, podcast-listening, party planning and magazine-loving kind of gal. When not with my family, you can usually find me perusing a bookstore or any shop that sells inspirational or creative items.

I enjoy all things uplifting and always look for ways to improve myself in areas that I am lacking. I never wanted to settle at being less than I can be. I am always on the prowl for a helpful tip or suggestion on how to improve my life.

But what I especially enjoy is having meaningful conversations with others about lessons we've learned along the way and sharing tips on how to do things better. I love the back-and-forth exchange of information that can help us "live our best lives" as Oprah Winfrey often says. I am still a big fan of hers and she is a role model on how to use your passion toward helping others to make a positive difference in the world. This little book comes out of that place of wanting to do exactly that.

I've learned through the years that wanting to better myself can sometimes turn into chasing after a picture-perfect life that is only attainable in the magazines. You end up never satisfied. I am still passionate about reading magazines, but I have learned through the years to use what I see in the media and magazines as only inspiration. To not treat it as the exact blueprint of what will work for *my* life.

When I was younger, I felt I could never achieve the vision I saw in the magazines or inside my head. I had to fight those annoying inner voices saying that I wasn't this enough or that enough. For years, I used to think that it was ok that I wasn't content in the moment because I knew for a fact that the future was always going to be better. Someday it indeed would be perfect!

Yes, I wanted everything to look a certain way and long before Martha Stewart came onto the scene, I was obsessed in my early 20's with the idea of having matching everything - like the perfect dinner place setting or bathroom ensemble.

I remember being in college thinking I couldn't wait to graduate and have money so I could have my own apartment and afford a beautifully coordinated bedroom and bathroom. By then I would surely feel grown up and successful.

Ok, I know you are probably snickering by now thinking - *that poor girl, did she really think that life would fit neatly into a pretty box with a colorful bow?* Excuse me but yes, I did! And it was that way of thinking that led me down a not-so-happy road of marrying the wrong guy at 23 (we were complete opposites and not in a good way). My thought was that it would help me feel more grown up. Or at least I thought.

It also contributed to me being a people pleaser for years and chasing after that picture-perfect life that would never come. Thankfully, I pursued a public relations career that utilized my natural strengths of writing, speaking and event planning, and I steadily worked my way up the corporate ladder. I just wish I could have had my personal life more on track back then!

If only I could have had the opportunity to talk to my 20-year-old self and tell her what I know now decades later. I would say to her that she really *did* know what was best for her life and to stop looking to others to tell her what to do or how to be. I would have told her to listen to advice from others, but ultimately follow her intuition of what to keep in her life. Also, I would have said to keep things simple, and not try to do everything and be all things to all people.

I would have also said to not be so trusting of every person who comes into her life because there will be people who will hurt her emotionally. In most cases, it will not be because they are bad people, but because they haven't dealt with their own issues and insecurities. Instead of making those people confidants, she should keep them at a distance and always guard her heart. Lastly, I would have advised her to embrace her uniqueness and follow the advice I am giving later in this book. I am getting ahead of myself so I will stop for now on continue with what led me to being in a withering place.

Flash forward - several years later. First an amicable divorce from the "wrong" guy, followed by some soul searching, therapy and a strong desire to settle down with a partner and become a mom. It was about a year before I found and married my true soul mate and became a mom to two beautiful girls. After eight years together, we relocated from the hustle-bustle of Orange County, CA to a nice upscale community, Ahwatukee. It is a lovely suburb of Phoenix.

We moved into a nearly 3,000 square foot dream home with a pool, big yard and a wonderful neighborhood with friendly neighbors. We lived within walking distance to an exceptional elementary and middle school. I worked as a part-time community reporter and volunteered in my girls' schools, and we later adopted two adorable mini dachshund puppies. I was living what many would call the "American dream" and all that was left to do was to live happily ever after – or so I thought!

Boy, I can see now how naïve I was back then in the way I viewed my life. I thought I had so much control over everything, and little did I know that the coming years would prove otherwise.

In fact, even with all the blessings I had in my life at that time, the reality was that the same inner issues that plagued me over the years remained. They didn't go away just because I had all the trappings of what American society says is supposed to make me happy.

It wasn't until I hit a series of difficulties in my life, that I could finally see that I needed to adjust the way I dealt with major change and uncertainty. While I was proud that I successfully dealt with an earlier divorce and then typical marriage struggles as well as a bout of post-partum depression with my second daughter, I had no idea of what was to come. How tested I would really feel.

Moving back to California

The long and short of it was my girls and I were enjoying living in Arizona and had no plans of moving back to California. But after five years, my husband was feeling the opposite. He missed the ocean and career opportunities in Southern California. He was struggling to find full-time permanent work in Arizona and was working as a contract IT project manager.

For a few years we were bickering back and forth about his unhappiness living in Arizona. He then wrote me a letter in 2009 telling me point-black about his strong desire (somewhat demand) to move back to California. By then I started to entertain the idea of going back, especially since our girls were getting older and I wanted them to have more options of where to go to college in-state.

However, I knew moving away from a life our girls enjoyed would be a big adjustment for them and they would have to leave a house and schools they loved. But one day I woke up and knew that the decision came down to my marriage or this move. It was like a scene from one of our favorite movies, the *Family Man.* Just like when Tea Leoni's character says to her husband Jack, Nicholas Cage's character, I said to my husband, *"I choose us"* and *"yes, we could move our family back to Orange County if he found a permanent job there."*

Little did I know exactly what that move would cost us financially, emotionally and everything else that happened along the way. Let's just say it was HUGE for me and my family. The series of events that followed shook me to my core.

During that period, we experienced major financial difficulties, lived apart for a year while he worked in California, and lost one of our dogs within days to valley fever. A few months later in early 2011, I lost one of my best friends to cancer (Sue) after being diagnosed only three months before.

Later in the year we found a family home to purchase but experienced a long escrow from hell, which resulted in living in a local hotel for a month while it got resolved. Then six weeks after we finally got settled, my husband contracted a fast-moving bacterial infection (flesh-eating disease) Christmas weekend. He was within a day of losing a limb or worse, it taking his life.

While another person may have had a difficult time with all those trials and changes but got through it ok, it was devastating for me and caused me to go into a debilitating depression. It shook my world and left me feeling uncertain about *everything.*

Once life finally settled down for my family and I was healed from my depression, I looked back and realized that not only did I survive that awful time in our lives but in many ways, I was forever changed in a positive way. For example, I was able to get a better handle of some internal issues that had dogged me for years. This included people pleasing, clutter and shame. By always looking forward and not losing hope (even though I had a few days when I practically did), I was ready to start blooming again when the time was right.

Writing this very personal book is my way of using the pain I went through to hopefully help others who are feeling the way I did back then. It is such a pleasure for me to share with a bigger audience these lessons and stories that I have told to my girlfriends for years. As a professional writer and storyteller and forever student of self-improvement, I want to use these natural gifts to to help those who need a boost of light and encouragement to get going again after an especially tough time.

Now let's get started on nine ways I started to bloom again, which helped me go from withering to FLOURISHING!

CHAPTER ONE

Start with a New Vision

A gardener learns more from his mistakes than his successes

—Barbara Dodge

It was Father's Day weekend 2010, and that was the last time I remember feeling free and easy and happy in the present before the craziness of our life began. We were up in Sedona, AZ visiting one of our favorite places on earth and celebrating my husband's last weekend in Arizona, before moving to California to start his new job. I kept my promise to move back to California if he found a permanent job there. We decided to live apart while the girls finished one more year of school in Arizona. We were about to turn the page on a new chapter of our lives.

Looking back, I wanted that weekend to last forever. I remember feeling especially fit and healthy after recently losing 10 pounds and having a great time as a family in such a beautiful and inspiring place. I kept thinking that this was how life was always supposed to feel, and I felt a lot of gratitude. In the months ahead, I would go back to that weekend in Sedona several times in my mind, asking myself why life couldn't go back to that happy place and time.

After we returned home, my husband got in his car that Sunday afternoon with his suitcase and box of essentials. I felt like I was sending off my first child to college. Honestly, everything right after that was a bit of a blur. I was left to live life as a single mom and keep our girls busy over that hot Phoenix summer and school year ahead. I

In addition to my mommy duties, I was also tasked with de-cluttering my home, packing up non-essential items, renovating my house to sell, and selling our house. I also was dealing with not only the emotions of missing my husband, but two angry daughters who didn't want to move.

There was also the worry of how we were going to pay for everything when I couldn't pursue client work since I needed to get our house ready for sale and take care of our young daughters. **To say I struggled during this phase of my journey would be a complete understatement.**

I felt the weight of everything I had to do before we could move to California and had an angry heart toward my husband.

An example of this was one Saturday in July. As I sat in the middle of my garage trying to go through years of clutter in the 110-degree summer weather, you can only imagine what I was thinking when my husband called me from Laguna Beach. He proceeded to tell me how lonely and bored he was on his only day off. Oh, how I would have traded loneliness and boredom with the ocean breeze on my face over dirty, sweaty and exhausted going through the junk in our garage and caring for our girls!

I kept denying the fact that this was really happening and kept hoping it was all a dream, rather a nightmare. I hoped I would wake up soon. But in hindsight, I wish I would have accepted my new reality sooner and created a new vision for myself to work toward. I wish I was not so emotional about everything - especially since we were just at the start of many more challenges to come.

If your trials were or are anything like mine, which was dealing with many changes and losses at one time, or something far greater and more painful, it's easy to get stuck in the "why" of it all. Why me or why that person who I love? Why do I have to go through this now? Why didn't God answer my prayers for this problem to be solved?

That question certainly came up six months later when I was flying out to say goodbye to my dear friend Sue in California. She had been diagnosed with cancer a few months earlier and was told by her doctor that she only had a few weeks to live. I asked God, why take someone in the prime of her life? She had two little children, a loving husband, amazing parents and brother and so many friends who adored her. Why this woman?! No explanation could ever be an acceptable reason why. But I now realize that sometimes we find the why out much later- or never at all.

Create a new life from a blank canvas

If you went through a big life change or dealt with a major loss, what I have learned is to not take your old life and mold it to fit around your new one. Better to put the best memories of your old life in a scrapbook or memory box (virtual or literal) that you can bring up whenever you want. Then, start with a fresh mound of clay to create a new life based on your different set of circumstances.

It's like when we moved into our California home. The prior owners had a rose garden in a sunny corner of the side back yard. Whe we moved into the house, it had been neglected for quite some time and had seen better days. At first, I tried to plant flowers around some of the existing roses and roots of other ones, hoping they would come back. Whatever I did, it never looked right.

After finally giving in a year later and deciding to start anew, my husband completely removed everything from the garden and tilled the soil to give me a blank canvas to start with. We planted new seedlings, breathing life into that space. The once beautiful rose garden had now become a useful herb garden. Both approaches worked well, but for our family the latter suited us best!

When you appreciate what you had before a loss but look ahead as having a blank canvas, your new reality has every chance to succeed because it isn't starting from what is *lacking*. Nothing is missing because it is what it is. It is like playing a game of poker and getting a new hand of cards. There is no mourning that prior set of cards you were dealt, because now you have a new set of cards to deal with. You have a fresh set of circumstances to create something entirely new that fits who you are now.

I wish I would have understood that concept sooner during our transitional period. I made the mistake of allowing myself to stay in a negative place of going over and over in my mind how much we had lost financially with my husband living away for a year. We also had to sell our Arizona home at a loss, which sadly included giving up most of our new furniture as part of the deal.

And then before getting settled back in California, we had to move several times in those first six months.

But what was far worse than that was the fact that my new reality in California would not include my beautiful friend Sue. She died four months before we moved back to the community right next to hers. Holding on to what was supposed to be and comparing that to my current reality (which was a series of disappointments and struggles) was too much to bear at times.

Just before the first anniversary of my girlfriend's passing, one of the things that really helped me to move on from sadness every time I thought of her was changing my thoughts. Instead of thinking and mourning what I had lost, I changed my thoughts to feeling grateful for what I had. I thanked God that I was able to know Sue and have a wonderful friendship for 15 years. I would take that any day over **not** having the extreme blessing of being her friend.

Do we ache for those we love who are no longer with us? Of course! But we can be thankful for the time we had with them and rejoice in that thought, rather than sit in sadness wishing things were different.

We can complain because rose bushes have thorns or rejoice because thorn bushes have roses.

-- Abraham Lincoln

I had another mind shift that was reinforced when I heard Pastor Rick Warren's first sermon back at Saddleback Church after losing his 27-year-old son four months earlier. Warren is the author of the book, *The Purpose Driven Life*. He said that all of us either know someone in the middle of a crisis, are in a crisis ourselves, or about to go into one. I finally accepted the fact that a smooth and easy road of life is promised to no one and that we must find a way to feel joy and contentment in between, and even *during,* the tough times.

When I looked at it that way, I knew that I needed to not only be strong for the tough times (even if it was just a difficult day or week). I needed to feel joy in between and *during* the tough times whenever possible. I realized that my new vision for myself would be a life that would be joyful no matter what challenges would come my way. I would teach my family to do the same.

Pastor Rick's wife Kay shared a perfect example of this when she also spoke during that first sermon back after her son died. She said that the day she and her husband found out their son Mathew had taken his life after a life-long struggle with mental illness, she showed her husband the necklace she was wearing that said *choose joy.* It was a small gesture, but she wanted her husband to know that no matter what, they would still find joy in whatever challenges they faced. And this included even if it was the worst of the worst—losing a child. Kay is the author of the book *Choose Joy…. Because Happiness isn't Enough.*

Building a new life after divorce

On a much smaller scale, going through a divorce in my early 30's was a difficult time for me. It was a situation in my life that I felt I handled rather well considering I didn't see it coming. I thought I had my life plan all figured out. I met my first husband while away at college when I was 20. After 10 years together (six years married), our lives were going in completely different directions. In the end, it came down to me wanting to have a child and my ex still feeling like one! I remember about a month before my 30th birthday, I could feel a change was on the horizon. At the time, I was thinking maybe it involved getting a bold sassy haircut. Little did I know that the big change coming would be a divorce!

After we decided to separate a few weeks later, I remember deciding to not let wasting a decade with the wrong guy get in the way of having a happy future. I remember thinking I didn't want to emerge from the divorce being a bitter person who never wanted to risk falling in love again.

Granted, I didn't have children with this man and that certainly would have complicated matters significantly. Even still, my divorce left me broken at the time and it could have easily hardened me. I could have been bitter with no desire to give love a second chance. Instead, I allowed time to heal my wounds and waited until I was ready to get back into the dating game again.

It was hard and I often felt lonely and sad when I would see couples with children at the grocery store on a Saturday evening, wondering if marriage and kids would ever be in the cards for me.

Once the time felt right to start moving forward as a newly single woman, I counted my blessings. This included having great friends, a fulfilling career and owning my own condo. Instead of having a specific plan for my life to follow, I looked ahead as if it was an adventure. It was ok that for the first time, I didn't know where my journey would lead. Now that was a first for me. I let go of the old vision of my life and accepted quite early on that wherever life took me, I was going to be ok.

I headed out that brand new year in 1994 with the goal of eventually marrying again and having children. I was also open to the idea of supporting myself as a single woman and being fixed up by friends and went on dates with interesting people I met. I also joined a tennis club and started friendships with single women who were also starting new phases of their lives.

When I got my divorce decree in the mail that December, I sent a Christmas card to my ex. It included a note saying that I truly forgave him for the hurt he caused me and the part that I contributed to as well. I said that we both could move forward with no regrets when it came to our relationship. He later thanked me for that letter and said it gave him peace and helped him to move on.

For me, it was just the push I needed to fully embrace life without him. One month later, I met the man I was meant to be with forever at the tennis club we both belonged to. We met at a Super Bowl party that the tennis club was hosting on Super Bowl Sunday 1995. After a year of dating, we couldn't wait to get married, buy a home, start a family and share our life together. Exactly three years later, on Super Bowl Sunday 1998, at about the same time we first met right before kickoff, our first baby daughter was born. Although I had a general goal in mind after my divorce, I let life unfold without trying to control it, and I got the best possible results.

It's ok to feel like a seedling again

It's humbling to start fresh. It takes a lot of courage. But it can be invigorating. Put your ego on a shelf and tell it to be quiet.

--Jennifer Ritchie Payette

One thing to keep in mind as you create a new vision for

yourself is that it is ok to feel nervous about being a newbie again, now that your situation has changed. For example, you might be going back to work after being out of the job market for a long while. You now need to contribute to the family budget due to a financial crisis or divorce.

Or you might be dating again after a divorce or a spouse passing away. That was the case for me many years ago. After being with my ex-husband throughout my entire 20's, I found dating uncomfortable at first. Boy - did the guys change from their early 20's to their 30s! It was scary to me, but I embraced my new situation. It certainly helped me to adjust to it sooner.

Later in 2013, I went back into the corporate world after being away for more than a decade working as a remote freelance writer while raising our girls. It was scary and exhilarating at the same time. The year before, I learned new work skills like blogging and social media. It was a whole new ball game, and I certainly felt like a seedling with all the technical knowledge I needed to learn.

But once I got the basics down and studied quite a bit on the subject, I was confident to start a side blog of my own while also dipping my toes back into the corporate world again. I loved being back in the career I had prior to having children.

Tragedy and tough times can certainly change our situations and take away from us what is comfortable and what we have always known. But learning new things can stretch our minds and encourage us to be more curious about life. It sure did in my case and as you will read later, I'm not the most patient person when it comes to a learning curve.

Why not create a vision for yourself that stretches you and gives you butterflies in your stomach - especially if it was a long time ago when you felt them? Whatever it is that you are starting out new again, don't worry if you don't know exactly what you are doing at first. Embrace it as something positive. Remember that even the most beautiful rose or stunning flower once started as a seed and then a seedling before growing into its full glory!

Questions to ask yourself:

- ❖ What are you going to miss the most about your old reality?

- ❖ What are the positives of your new reality?

- ❖ If you were to create a memory box of items that represent your old life, what would it include?

- ❖ What are ways you can honor your past while celebrating your present?

CHAPTER TWO

Dig Up Shame

Shame needs three things to grow exponentially - secret, silence and judgment

—Brené Brown, PhD, author of *Daring Greatly*

I first learned about researcher Brené Brown when my sister Michelle emailed me the link to her popular vulnerability speech shown on TED Talks. By 2020, her speech has been viewed more than 45 million times, so it obviously struck a chord with a lot of people. Through her extensive research, she has brought the concepts of shame and vulnerability to the forefront and discusses how it affects the way we connect with others.

Since I have been studying happiness and connection for a decade now, I will never forget the first time I heard her speak on this topic. It was a lightning bolt moment for me, not just professionally but personally. I finally had a name to one of the things preventing me from finally moving on from a difficult two-year period. I was able to fully accept myself in a loving way.

I also related to the way she did public speaking. I like how she reveals a lot about herself in her talks and it's what I like to do as well. She talks about how public speaking didn't initially come naturally to her but the impact of her vulnerability in her talks on others has been absolutely mind blowing.

What is shame? According to Brown, shame is that dark feeling inside when we think something about ourselves makes us unworthy, unlovable and not deserving of true connection with others. Brown states that as human beings we are hard-wired for connection and love. When we feel unloved and unworthy, we are susceptible to things like addiction, depression and suicide.

Dealing with lingering shame was one of the best things I did to help me bloom again and move on from my depression. It changed how I dealt with people who tried to shame me. It also helped me to be more authentic in the way I present myself to others. Removing shame is essential to having strong social bonds, which is not only important in times of crisis. Science shows that it is a key component to living a happy life. Writing about happiness and connection has become one of my life's missions (see Chapter 8) and discussing shame is a part of that education.

Shame is a soul eating emotion

−C. G Jung

To see if you have shame that might be holding you back from moving forward after a tough time, ask yourself this question and fill in the blank. I feel like I am less than others or embarrassed because of my _____.

For some it could be their weight, an illness, divorce, education level, relationship issues, ethnicity, difficult upbringing, past sexual abuse, financial situation, disability, sexual orientation, mistakes made, uneventful life, work issues, misbehaved children. You name it and you can feel ashamed by it.

Shame is what prevents you from making a change because you think your background, challenges or past mistakes make you unworthy to be the best version of yourself.

Shame is also what people use against you to keep you down. I've made the mistake of allowing this to happen too long from a few people. Once I understood what shame was and removed that way of thinking, it changed my relationships with people in a wonderfully positive way.

It is not an easy topic to discuss, and I am forever grateful to Brown for taking on this subject with such vigor and communicating it in terms that people can understand.

Shame played a role in my life when I allowed others to judge me on everything from my parenting skills to decisions I made. I allowed others (not many, but one is enough) to make me feel less than because I had to downsize to a small fixer upper home in high-priced South Orange County. I also felt shame around some people when I had to drive an old car way past its prime because we lost a lot of money during our move back to California.

I even allowed someone close to me to define my life as a series of mistakes or put down my husband's mistakes. We know realistically that we are no different than any other couple in that we have had ups and downs in life, but I let that person shame me. What matters is that my heart and life are full now. I wouldn't trade anything for the wisdom I have gained through every experience and challenge I've endured.

Once they know they've got a hold of your shame, they can shake it out and hold it up for the all the world to see. And you become less than it. You become something disgusting."

–Kirsty Eagar, Raw Blue

Instead of feeling shame of going through what I've gone through or the choices I have made in my life, I feel an amazing sense of courage. I had confidence knowing that nothing would bring me down and make me feel less than others. It's easy to go back in your mind and beat yourself up for things of your past. But honestly, where is that going to get you?

Learn the lesson you need to learn and then hold your head up high and stand firmly on the ground knowing you are a survivor. Hopefully you will even get to a point where you can share your story with others to help them deal with *their* shame as I hope to do with this book.

According to Brown, when we keep our shame a secret and/or allow others to use it as a weapon against us, we become susceptible to addiction. And we live in a highly addicted society. In her research, she found that people with unresolved shame often numb their pain with food, medications, drugs, alcohol, shopping or other destructive behaviors. It gives them relief and alters their reality. But as we all know, it is a temporary solution and all you are left with is another problem - the addiction to deal with.

You can throw away the need to be perfect and feel good that you are deserving of love exactly as you are

However, when you dig up your shame and bring it into the

light, it no longer has power over you. It becomes a part of your survivor story and something you acknowledge and have learned from. You can throw away the need to be perfect and feel good that you are deserving of love exactly as you are.

When you realize that your life is only for <u>you</u> to live, you will no longer put up with others who judge you. Sure, they may do it behind your back, but you can't control that. I can assure you they are judging you because of their own unresolved shame.

When you realize your life is only for you to live you will no longer put up with others who judge you

Isn't that a huge relief? It sure was for me. Now to get there, you need a few trustworthy people in your life and for some, a professional counselor to work through your feelings. There are also great books and videos available that discuss shame, and I would start with Brown's research. I was and still am fortunate to have a close inner circle of friends and family who helped me sort through my feelings. They were also the ones who helped give me the last kick in the butt to move forward and leave my tough period behind and see it only in the rear-view mirror.

Shame in action

I knew a friend who had a difficult childhood and was raised by a cruel grandmother who often shamed her and made her feel like she was less than others. It resulted in my friend growing up with people-pleasing tendencies. She was also hypersensitive to people putting her down or bringing up any of her past mistakes, which were no more significant than the average person's.

Before she made a big change in her life and finally dug up the shame and got rid of it, she had an experience that really shook her. It was one fall when she and her husband had a conflict with one of the parents on their child's sports team where her husband was the coach. The parent was being obnoxious about how he disliked her husband's coaching style and was up in my friend's face about it. He figured he was entitled since she was the coach's wife. When she pushed back, he made it personal.

He brought up things about her and her husband's reputation. While not true, it still triggered terrible feelings of shame and basically turned her life upside down whenever she had to deal with him or his wife. So, she verbally fought back.

The tensions escalated to the point that one day when she was in her car on the phone with someone raging about the situation, she ran out of gas on a side road, not too far from her home.

She was so immersed talking on the phone with a friend about the parents who were shaming her that she left her car in the middle of the road. She started walking down the street to her house. She was oblivious to the fact that she left her keys in the ignition, purse on the passenger seat along with a half-eaten burrito. Not only was the car unlocked but one of the doors was left open.

She was caught up in the moment of discussing how awful this man was to her. Imagine her surprise when she made the 30-minute walk home and there were police cars in her driveway, a helicopter hovering over her house and a husband completely bewildered by it all.

The police officer thought she was escaping her car for domestic reasons and was ready to haul both she and her husband down to police headquarters.

Have you ever been so immersed in a negative situation that it takes over your life? That is what shame can do to you when someone uses it against you and my advice is to not let it get to that point. Rid any shame on your own terms, so you never have to worry about being swept away by it.

When you do that, you can face the world being authentically you and you will be amazed at how people react to you. Being real without worry of being condemned is refreshing and it allows people to be their real selves back to you. Wouldn't it be great if everyone could stop pretending that they have everything figured out. If you do encounter someone who is uppity and acts like they are better than you or tries to judge you, just smile. Because you know you are a simply fabulous person who is loved as you are. Then be on your way—far away from them.

Embrace vulnerability

When we get rid of our shame, we are free to embrace being vulnerable and all the good that comes with that. What is vulnerability? Again, Brown describes it best by saying vulnerability is uncertainty, risk and emotional exposure. What that meant to me was to allow myself to really be seen for who I was. And being afraid of people judging me or telling me that I was not good enough as I was.

When I got to my 20's, I had such extremes in my life of people close to me who were either confirming what I thought about myself (which was positive and loving) against those who used my vulnerabilities against me to put me down to feel better about themselves. I loved them so I believed their lies instead of embracing that I did not need to be perfect to be successful and happy. Especially when you are married to someone doing that to you, it can cause havoc in your life. While my first marriage is a closed chapter in my life and something I fully healed from, I think it is important to share a part of that story to help others.

I was married to a man who was three years older than me and very opinionated. He would say what he thought was the best way to be, look and feel. The funny thing is that it always seemed completely opposite of who I was - talk about a mind trip! We started out as friends and were attracted to each other's differences.

Wanting to feel grown up in the worst way when I was in my early 20's, I married this man. I later found out, he was not "my person" and was not someone I could grow old with. When he and I finally broke up, I was able to truly be free to be me and find a life partner who accepted me as I was but also encouraged me to grow and be the best person I could be.

For example, when I mentioned to my ex about writing a book someday, he scoffed and said, *"what in the world could you write about that people would want to read, let alone pay for?"* Compare that to my husband of today whose response was, *"I can totally see you doing that, and I will help you get there."* Surround yourself with people who will go there with you and believe in you as much as you believe in yourself.

Embracing vulnerability later in life, especially after going through a difficult two-year period with my family, has been simply amazing to me. I hope others will be inspired to do so after reading this chapter. It means going out on a limb and loving with all your heart even knowing that you might get hurt. It means pursuing a passion of yours that you never thought you could do and giving yourself permission to try even if you don't know if it will work. It is exposing a part of yourself that may resonate with others (or maybe not) but it doesn't matter because you are just being you and no longer need the approval of others.

The result for me is a deeper happiness and contentment that I never knew I could have. Even now when I have days that seem out of control or uncertain or when there are a lot of negativities around me, I can still find things to laugh and be happy. I live as if everything is good—because honestly it is. There is always someone worse off than you and if you have another day on this earth then I say truly embrace it! I learned the hard and long way that getting rid of shame and embracing vulnerability can literally set your soul free!

Questions to ask yourself:

- ❖ Do you have one or more things about yourself you feel shameful about?

- ❖ Is there a person in your life who makes you feel shame when you are with him or her? Can you limit the time you spend with that person?

- ❖ Is there a trustworthy person or professional who you can confide in who will bring light to your shame so you can finally get rid of it?

- ❖ Do you have a bad habit that you do to numb the pain you feel from shame? What is your plan to stop doing it?

CHAPTER THREE

Sprinkle Seeds of Humor

The most wasted day is one without laughter

--C.C. Cummings

The funny thing about laughter is it is seriously one of the best things you can do to give yourself breathing room when you are going through tough times. I really learned the power of humor that first Thanksgiving after we moved out of our family home in Arizona to a condo down the street.

My husband was home visiting for a few days and the girls really missed their dog who went to doggy heaven five weeks earlier. They also missed our other dog we gave to another family when she couldn't handle all the changes going on in our family and was lashing out at everyone.

This year we were not able to spend the holiday with either of our parents or siblings in different states and the holiday didn't feel the same. Instead of gathering around our big family table, we sat around a small bistro table in the middle of our small living area, eating a prepared dinner from Mimi's Café.

Everyone seemed quiet and a bit sad as we went around the small table giving thanks for the good things we had in our lives. Of course, we knew logically that we had many blessings to be thankful for, but our hearts felt heavy from all the things that were different this Thanksgiving. When it was my turn to give thanks, I pointed out that I felt especially thankful for having a family that is naturally funny and makes me laugh, especially during difficult times.

I wish you could have seen how they all sat up after I said that and got these big smiles on their faces. It was like watching a wilted flower come back to life after watering it. They started telling favorite jokes and we all thought shared silly moments we had as a family. It completely changed the mood for the better. I look back on that Thanksgiving and all I remember was eating a delicious dinner and enjoying quality time with our little family. On top of that - no dishes to clean.

I can't say it enough about how thankful I am to be married to a man who laughs easily and likes to be silly at times. My husband Brian often reminds us of the funny and loveable father character, Phil Dunfey, on ABC's popular funny sitcom Modern Family. We were so sad to see it end in 2020. I'd be lying if I said I always embrace his silliness but for the most part, I just love that he makes me smile and laugh. He says that part of his personality came from his grandpa. I think it is great that my daughters got his sense of humor as well.

A good laugh is sunshine in the house

--William Makepeace Thackeray

As I get older, I like to laugh more. I think it is more important than ever to try and seek out ways to find humor in things especially when there is so much heartache in the news. Things feel so heavy at times. Ever since 9/11, it seems like we are on high alert all the time. That's why I'm a big fan of sitcom comedies that make me feel like I just took a happy pill after watching an episode.

I shared the importance of laughter with my family and when I had a milestone birthday a year later, my family gave me one of my favorite gifts of all time – a happy box. It was a silver square gift box that featured a favorite family photo on each side of the cube and engraved on the top. While that was precious enough, inside they included an individual piece of paper for each birthday year I was celebrating.

On each paper was a memory of something funny that happened in the past to our family and makes us laugh even today. They even remembered and included funny stories I shared with them years ago from my past before I had a family. It's a gift that keeps on giving because I pull it out whenever I need to be reminded that everything will be ok no matter how hard something seems right now. I know it can happen because the stories I share later in this chapter were all included in my happy box, even though at the time happiness was the last emotion I was feeling! It is a wonderful gift to make and give to someone you love, or maybe even for yourself.

According to WebMD, laughing does several positive things to our bodies. It exercises our facial muscles so after a hearty laugh, we feel less stressed and more relaxed. Laughing releases good-feeling endorphins and like running, it helps us sleep better. Laughing also burns calories. When we have a good laugh with those we care about or want to get to know better, it helps the bonding process, and you feel more connected to them.

Another way my husband and I add more laughter to our lives is when we catch a show at the Improv Comedy Store on occasion. Some of our favorite comedians are Sebastian Maniscalco and Craig Shoemaker, who bring so much joy to people. They have made it their life's mission to make people laugh and lighten their thoughts even if only for a few hours.

I remember my husband taking me out on a Thursday night after a tough week living in a hotel and not knowing when and if we could move into our new home. We felt like kids that night and laughed so hard my face hurt (exercising those facial muscles) and my stomach ached in the best way.

It was just what we needed to keep going when it would be weeks before we finally closed escrow on our home.

Bad experiences we look back now and laugh

That summer when my husband moved to California for his job and we were alone in Phoenix, trying to find the humor in crazy situations was not something I did very well.

Once I started to ease up on expecting everything to go perfectly, laughing about funny situations certainly helped me in my recovery.

It really helps when we can take ourselves less seriously and realize that life is life and some things you can't control. Here are some funny situations I can laugh at now, but at the time not so much.

The scorpion "monster"

It was that first Monday my husband had moved away, and my girls and I woke up to find the largest scorpion we had ever seen since moving to Arizona. It was lying in the middle of our foyer, fully alive and scary looking. Without my husband around (aka the scorpionator) to get rid of that creepy critter, all us girls could do was to throw a bunch of shoes and scream loudly at it hoping it would just explode from all the excitement and die. Heck, I never had to deal with a scorpion on my own before!

We eventually found a big heavy boot in the garage to kill it, and its crushed body stayed on the bottom of that boot until the bug guy came weeks later for our regular service and kindly removed it. It is funny now but at the time you would have thought I was wrestling an alligator!

Meet the teacher night

That same week after my husband left for California, I had to clean the pool right before Meet the Teacher Night. It was the only time I could do it since our realtor open house was scheduled for early the next morning. I was running super late so with full makeup and outfit on, I grabbed the long pool brush (looks like a six-foot toothbrush) and proceeded to do my best, not really knowing what I was doing since cleaning the pool had always been my husband's job.

As I was finishing up the last corner of the pool, I slipped and fell in our pool right before we had to leave.

I ran in the house, reapplied my makeup as best I could in 90 seconds, combed my hair and put it up in a nice bun, and threw on a new tank top and skirt. I then yelled at the kids to get in the car, and we made it to the school just in time with no one the wiser.

However, you can imagine my embarrassment when I discovered that, because I didn't have time to change my brassiere, I was saying hello to other parents and the new teacher completely unaware that I had big damp clingy circles around my ta-ta's. Oh yes, I found that out as I was leaving the open house, and my neighbor mentioned it to me as we were leaving. That still makes me laugh but you know what—that was my life back then…just surviving and getting through the day.

Underdressed and over embarrassed at the wake

Another funny but embarrassing situation, also involving clothing, occurred the second summer we moved to California. I'm not proud of this story and can't believe I am including it, but it was such a great lesson of finding the humor in crazy situations. I was still in my healing process, which is probably why it affected me the way it did because the rest of my family barely reacted to it -- only to my overreaction of the situation.

It was Father's Day 2012 and after a time when I was not being realistic of my time and energy resources and had completely overcommitted myself (more about this in Chapter 4), I was feeling particularly burned out. On the spur of the moment, my family and I decided to relax at the beach on my husband's special day. Life had been going way too fast for us for several weeks and there weren't a lot of clean clothes options. We grabbed whatever we could find to wear over our bathing suits and made the drive down to the beach. What everyone was wearing was the least of my worries. I just wanted to get there and veg out.

On the way to the beach, my husband's friend, whose father had passed away a few days before, left us voicemail. From what we gathered, we believed he was having a few friends over at his brother's home to keep him company as he grieved on Father's Day, and he asked if we could stop by. It was down the street from the beach, and we lived in the opposite direction. We made the decision that when we were done at the beach, we would gather our things and make our way to our friend's brother's home in Newport Coast.

As we walked up to his brother's beautiful and palatial home, we heard people talking in the backyard, so we went in through the side gate thinking they were out barbequing. Within minutes, we could see that this was no casual gathering - it was the wake after our friend's father's funeral!

Picture this—it looked like a scene from a lavish party on *The Real Housewives of Orange County* show on Bravo. The home had a stunning and lush backyard with sweeping views of the Pacific Ocean from its balcony and people were nicely dressed—certainly no one looked like they had just come from a day spent at the beach! Contrast that to my family who stood there wearing sand-soaked mismatched clothing, matted hair and flip flops. I think one of us even had mismatched flip flops. Even my normally stylish 10-year-old fashionista looked like she was ready to join the circus.

Looking back, what we should have done was go back to the car and have my husband find our friend and give him a big hug as well as his wife and mother and be on our way because we were completely underdressed for a wake. But instead, at the urging of my family, we stayed for the next hour or so. The whole time I felt ashamed and embarrassed thinking that my family's "outer" look matched what I was feeling inside at that time - out of control, out of place and not at all at our best or anywhere near it.

Under different circumstances, I probably wouldn't have felt so bad but in hindsight, I wish we had left after seeing our friend and then on the way home had a good laugh about how silly we looked.

Instead, I let the situation devastate me and dominate the next few hours because I couldn't stop berating my family about it—reliving the embarrassment over and over instead of just trying to find the humor in it.

I try now to be more light-hearted and find humor where I used to find embarrassment. When I started to seek out more humor in my life, my girlfriend and I had a fun time setting up my husband for a *Candid Camera* or *Punked* moment.

My short-lived clown career

In addition to working as a professional writer my entire career, I have always been an imaginative type and love thinking of ways to turn my hobbies or creative ideas into side money-making endeavors. From having a cookie business to professional organizing, let's just say that Shark Tank is one of our favorite television shows to watch.

I have so many ideas in fact that one of my best friends and husband love to tease me about it. They often use a phrase that they borrowed from another girlfriend of mine who was going through a period when she pursued many different endeavors that never really took off. One time when she was about to share yet another new idea to me and a mutual friend of ours over lunch, he looked at her and said, "What is it this time, clown college?" It's a phrase that my husband started saying to me as well in fun.

With that in mind, I decided to turn the tables and have a little fun with my husband. Picture me and my husband sitting together at a Dave Ramsey financial seminar held at Saddleback Church waiting for it to begin. As we were waiting, I shared with him in typical "Cher-like" unbridled passion how excited I was about a new business kit that I had ordered online to help with the family finances. At the time I wasn't working much, and we could certainly use the money, so he perked up as I started to tell him what it was.

I said that the kit was called *How to Become a Clown Balloon Artist in 5 Simple Steps*. Bless his heart, he wanted to be supportive and didn't interrupt me as I proceeded to tell him that the kit cost $300 and included several CD's, a clown wig, bazooka and balloons to practice with. I think he at first was envisioning me as a party planner and not as an actual balloon artist. Did he think I was going to be directing the clown?

One of my best friends Heather, who I met in Phoenix and urged me to do this, would have done just about anything to be sitting there watching my hubby's face as I told him about my "clown kit". How I wish I could have secretly videotaped it. He seemed to really believe what I was saying, and you could see it in his eyes that he was having a hard time processing the idea that his freelance writer wife was going to be dressed as a clown and doing balloon art.

I couldn't believe I didn't lose it and started laughing but he still seemed pretty convinced it was true up until the moment I told him that I scheduled my first gig in two weeks on a Friday night to dress up as a clown and work at the Irvine Spectrum. The Spectrum is an upscale outdoor shopping hub in Orange County, and we go there often with our girls. Of course, that was when he knew I was pulling his leg, and we had the best laugh after that. To make light of the situation and not take myself so seriously was when I knew I was on my way to a full recovery from my depression.

If you have been able to live a life without embarrassing or tough moments, then you are one of the lucky ones and I'm happy for you. But if your life is anything like mine, it is a series of crazy moments in between the regular ones and research shows that those who go with the flow more and laugh often increase their chances for a longer life. In fact, many seniors who live to 90 or older attribute having a good sense of humor as one of their longevity secrets.

It sure worked for comedians like Bob Hope and George Burns who died shortly after their 100th birthday, and Phyllis Diller and Carol Channing who both died in their late 90s. More recently, actress and comedian Betty White who celebrated her 98th birthday in 2020 and is as funny and naughty as ever!

Questions to ask yourself

❖ What are some of the crazier moments in your past that you can laugh about now? Can you share that story with others for a good laugh?

❖ What are the things that currently make you laugh—comedy shows, sitcoms, certain friends, books, movies, talk show hosts or comedians? Do you make time to watch them or spend more time with people who make you laugh?

❖ Do you have funny photos of you or you laughing with friends and/or family that you can frame and have on display at work or home? It can help remind you not to take life so seriously.

❖ April is National Humor Month—is there a way you can celebrate it each year doing something silly or funny with others?

CHAPTER FOUR

Grow at Your Own Pace (& Resources)

Adopt the pace of nature—her secret is patience

--Ralph Waldo Emerson

Patience is not something that has ever come easy to me. In fact, we still laugh about the time my husband was frustrated at my lack of patience, and he said, "Cher—you need more P-A-T-I-E-N-C-E!" I replied rather forcefully, "what do you mean I need more patience?" I didn't even recognize the word when he spelled it out. Now, when he thinks I am being impatient, he says that I need more patti-ence!

I have a hard time waiting for anything and it was no different when we moved back to California. When we moved into our new home in early November 2011, I expected to pick up exactly where I left off when the girls finished school the previous May in Arizona. The fact that everything had changed - our state, community, home, schools and activities seemed to escape me. Heck, just about everything was new including our dog.

I remember trying to figure out a way to host a fall-themed open house at the end of November for our friends and family. That was after moving into a neglected fixer upper home with few funds left to upgrade other than paint and flooring.

How I wished back then that the Property Brothers from HGTV could swoop in and take my neglected property and turn it into a beautiful showcase home like the one I had just remodeled back in Arizona. I prayed but they never came. The reality was we had no time, no money, little energy and our house was far from guest ready. *Hellooo. Earth to Cher—are you nuts?* Thankfully my husband nixed the fall open house idea within minutes.

I recall at that time looking enviously at other Orange County moms at my daughters' schools thinking I should be just like them, as they went along their daily lives, not missing a beat. Mine in contrast had been turned upside down for months on end. That was one of the biggest mistakes I made, and I say this to you - go at your own pace during or after a crisis and let everything evolve with time. If you try to control everything and strive for perfection, it will only frustrate you, depress you and make you feel like something is wrong with your life.

When you are going through a difficult period, it is not the time to judge yourself and be unrealistic of what you can accomplish given your resources. It applies not only during times of crisis but in everyday life as well. For women especially, I think we believe that we were born with superhuman powers. Yes, there are times when we need to get a lot done in a short period of time. But that should be the exception and not the rule. You will read later in this chapter how I have had to relearn this lesson repeatedly.

The old way of thinking is that if you commit to something in the future and your situation changes or you are hit hard with something, it doesn't matter. Just pull up your bootstraps and dig in and make it happen exactly as planned, regardless of the consequences.

That way of thinking is nonsense and old century because these days, there are more people, resources and technology to help than ever before. We can always get more help, adjust the planning, push a date back or rethink the whole commitment so we don't have to push ourselves past the point of no return. I don't say this lightly because I am a firm believer in keeping commitments. But now that I am wiser, I know and try to do better.

Out of all the chapters in this book, I have to say I still struggle with this concept the most. I want to incorporate a good speed for my life that allows me to finish what I need to do during the day as well as fit in the things that are beneficial to me as an individual and in my relationship with others and my community.

I used to wake up most mornings like a bullet shot out of a cannon and had a hard time being realistic of what I could accomplish during the day. By early evening, I would collapse from exhaustion. Only recently have I learned to be realistic about what will be on my daily to do list. In fact, I now choose three main tasks I want to accomplish and that is my focus. If I can fit in more, that is icing on the cake, but I don't set myself up for failure like I did before. In the evening, I now take the time to wind down before I retreat for the night.

I have learned to write a more manageable and shorter to-do list and give myself the time needed to accomplish each task. Unless it has a specific date to be completed, I look at tasks to be done by the week now and not the day. I learned this when I gave my husband a list of things to do. He did better when he could fit it around other similar tasks and have a week or at least a few days to complete my tasks instead of cramming it all in one day.

For many of us, we think that we can plow through anything just because we have it in our head that we CAN regardless of unexpected commitments, energy level, budget etc.

Not being realistic with party planning

An example of this was years ago when a good friend of mine at the time planned a Hawaiian-themed birthday party on a Sunday for her 10-year-old child. This happened to be the same weekend as an important professional event she was hosting the day before. She invited about 20 kids over for a pool party and had a caterer friend in town to help her make the food for both events.

While the Saturday event went off without a hitch, the birthday party on Sunday was way behind schedule and my girlfriend…well, she was exhausted!

An hour or so before the party, there was a lot left to do, especially the homemade dishes still to finish. Knowing that my friend was stressed to the max, I suggested that she order pizzas with pineapple and ham to go with the theme, have them delivered and call it a day.

Keep in mind that I am like her and enjoy making homemade food for parties too, but I have learned that if it is going to make you crazy, you need to adjust the plan.

By her reaction, you would have thought I told her to spray Cheese Wiz on saltine crackers for the main entrée. She had it in her mind to do a certain Polynesian style food spread for the party of 10-year old's and by golly, she was sticking to the plan!

Well, the story goes that when my frazzled friend ran out to pick up the balloons, she ended up hitting a car in the parking lot and it turned out to be a bad accident, throwing the rest of the day into even more of a tailspin. That is what can happen when we short-change ourselves and are not realistic about our personal resources of time and energy.

I had my own version of that concept when I originally planned to host my parent's 50th wedding anniversary party for the summer after we moved into our California home. We discussed plans for the party the summer before and I figured we would be in our new home surely by September. That would give me plenty of time with my sister to plan something special nine months later.

But as you read earlier, we didn't move in until November and we were still reeling from more financial challenges, the mess from a terrible escrow and a near-death scare for my husband at Christmas that left me especially traumatized. I had no idea that by mid-January, I would be staring at the wall feeling numb and zombie-like from depression.

But even by February, I was still charging ahead and refused to let my family know how difficult it would be for me to co-host the party as originally discussed. I not only wanted to keep the Saturday event as planned, but then considered adding a brunch event at my home for a large group of family members the Sunday morning *after* the event. I loved the idea of hosting at our house since we were back in California, but it would put enormous pressure on me and my husband to get many things done on my house within six months. Again, what was I thinking?

Finally, by April I had a mini (ok major) nervous breakdown at the thought of planning two big events over the summer. There was my parents' 50th wedding anniversary in June followed by my husband's 50th birthday in August. This was in addition to the pressure we were feeling having financial issues from me being depressed and not able to work. I wished I had been more truthful about my situation earlier on. Once I finally spoke up, we adjusted the plans, and I felt much better.

I'm happy to say the party turned out wonderful and was held at my sister and brother-in-law's lovely guest-ready house in San Diego and a festive restaurant nearby. Even though it looked different than what we had planned, it was a beautiful and memorable event, and the focus was on my parents' special milestone, and I was of the right mind to enjoy it.

A few months later, we had a fun and memorable party for my husband's 50th birthday. We downsized it from a big shindig to a smaller more intimate affair at a beautiful timeshare condo in Newport Coast. My husband's parents donated the room and co-hosted it with me and my older daughter and I put together a video presentation of his life that turned out beautifully. His tennis buddies and a few close family and friends were invited, and I made some of my specialty dishes and desserts. The evening was fun for all. We had so much gratitude that we were celebrating his life on his 50th and not mourning his death since we were so close to losing him nine months earlier.

A new job at a crazy pace

Unfortunately, my new-found ability to stay within my limits was tested shortly thereafter (hint - it didn't stick). I believe God allows that to happen to double check if you got the lesson before moving on to the next one. I know you would think I would have learned it once and for all, but it is something that I constantly struggle with even though I am better at it now.

Literally the week after the anniversary party, I got my first blogging job with a former client. I was thrilled to be writing again and started mid-week with an assignment to write five blog articles, which included key words for search engine optimization, on a variety of topics. I took to blogging immediately and found the challenge exhilarating. The next week my client gave me 10 blog articles to write but wanted me to also post them to various websites. This added a technical element I wasn't used to. I thought to myself, *"Hmm that went well - they loved my writing, I was being creative, learning something new and I get paid."* I was hooked.

The next week was Fourth of July week, and they asked if I could write 20, 400-word blogs to cover writers on vacation and they would do the posting for me. I had no idea how hard it would be, but the money was good, they paid me in advance, so I was game. As expected from my previous two weeks, those first 10 blog articles I wrote felt like sheer delight. After each blog article I wrote, I felt a satisfaction that reminded me of eating a rich, creamy and decadent truffle.

But as with anything, too much of a good thing can become a bad thing and writing 20 blogs in one week was way too much for me, especially with having kids home full time on summer break. It was a new job, and the pace was too fast. Soon the anxiety got to me, and I started to feel sick to my stomach, much like eating 20 rich truffles in one sitting.

Commitments are like chocolates. Have too many in too short a time will make you sick to your stomach

What was worse was that after that crazy week when I needed a day off for a mental break, I was assigned 23 more articles to write over the next month. I got it as I was still trying to finish the last three from the week before. That became the cycle. I never had an end because before I finished the assignments from the week or month before, I already had the list and money paid for the next assignment.

That would have been fine but for me, I had to work non-stop between my mom duties and writing creatively—it was all too much.

When I pushed back, my client didn't take it well and there was no turning back in my mind because we needed the money since I hadn't been working for a while. I also didn't want to disappoint her as a former client and friend, so I charged ahead thinking I was Super Writer Woman with a red cape and all!

But the reality was I was more like Lucy Ricardo in an *I Love Lucy* episode. The one where Lucy has a new job trying to manage the chocolates coming down the conveyer belt. When she couldn't wrap them fast enough, started stuffing them in her pockets and then in her mouth so she wouldn't get in trouble with her supervisor.

You might be thinking about now how much longer I could work at that crazy pace without losing my mind. Turns out about three more weeks. By the end of July, I had written 63 blog articles in five weeks. The work included writing on different topics and posting them on several websites, adding a tech element that added more time. I basically felt like roadkill. I was writing from the moment I woke up at 5 a.m. until late in the evening, with no days off. In between the writing, I was taking my kids out to do summer activities.

My Watermelon Story

Thankfully a break came at the end of July when my bestie Heather and her family came out to visit us from Arizona and we had a nice night out with our husbands. The next day they asked me to join them for a day at the beach and all I could think about was how I would miss a day of writing. With my deadline looming, I thought to myself, *"Please don't pry me away from my computer."*

I eventually gave in. As I started to pack up the cooler, I picked up a clear bag containing a watermelon that was cut in half. At that moment, I literally could not decide if I should put it in my cooler as is (and cut it up at the beach) or slice it up before I left. My mind and body were so depleted that all I could do was stand there with a knife in my hand and start sobbing because I had no energy to make one simple decision.

As I babbled on about the watermelon to her husband, he safely removed the knife from my hand and placed me in the car with everyone ready to go. I was hoping they were indeed taking me to the beach and not dropping me off first at the psych ward of the nearest hospital!

Being the good friends that they were, they stopped at a supermarket and picked up food and drinks for all of us and a new magazine for me because they know me well. Off we went to the beach for a wonderful day of sun, fresh air and rejuvenation. They stepped in and helped me in a crisis moment, and we talked about it later. I never felt any judgment from them. That is an example of true friendship.

It gave me the break I needed, and I was able to slow down my pace as much as my client would allow. However, after a few months, I ended the job when I could clearly see that it was not the right pace for me at that point in my life. Instead of feeling bad about making a mistake in taking that job, I was thankful for the opportunity and the money and realized it was part of my new career path into the world of blogging, for clients as well as myself.

Questions to ask yourself:

❖ What are some situations that you overcommitted yourself? Did you go through with it or adjust the plans? How would you do it differently next time?

❖ Are you realistic about how much you can comfortably accomplish in a day? Are you able to leave things for the next day and not feel guilty?

❖ Do you give yourself time to truly think about if you can do something or do you say yes right away and then regret it later?

❖ Do you take breaks to give your mind a rest during the day? What can you start doing now to build in rest stops during the day for yourself?

CHAPTER FIVE

Prune Back What Doesn't Fit Anymore

"A simple life is not seeing how little we can get by with — that's poverty — but how efficiently we can put first things first. When you're clear about your purpose and your priorities, you can painlessly discard whatever does not support these, whether it's clutter in your cabinets or commitments on your calendar

— Victoria Moran, *Lit from Within: Tending Your Soul for Lifelong Beauty*

When a close girlfriend and I attended a *You Can Do It* conference in the spring of 2007, I remember one of the overriding themes we kept hearing was that the key to happiness and clarity is to simplify and de-clutter your life. From the late Dr. Wayne Dyer to Marianne Williamson, Cheryl Richardson to Deepok Chopra, these wise teachers all devoted at least part of their discussion to the importance of keeping things simple and getting clutter out of our lives.

Especially when you are going through tough times, dealing with clutter from the past, as well as the things that need to be dealt with daily can create a whole new set of issues if you don't get a grip on it. If you have ever watched an episode of *Hoarders* on TLC, you know what I mean.

Hoarder-level clutter can damage your health, relationships, self-esteem and much more. I used to watch that show a lot in the past to inspire me to work through my own garage clutter. I liked it because compared to the people on the show, mine seemed more manageable to deal with so it motivated me.

Hoarding is often triggered by a traumatic event

Of all the times I watched the show *Hoarders,* I clearly saw that more times than not, the hoarding was triggered or went into overdrive when the person experienced a traumatic event. The event could be a death of a family member, difficult divorce, major health issue or other life-changing event. Compulsive hoarding can happen to anyone. Some had a history of hoarding their entire lives and others showed no prior sign of hoarding tendencies until something happened to trigger that behavior.

Most people do not let their clutter get to a hoarder level, but there are many who have clutter that is weighing them down and preventing them from living a life that is focused on what is important to them *now*. If that is you, I know personally that it is not easy to let go of things from our past, but it is an important task to help you move on and embrace your new life.

For me, I was forced to deal with my clutter once and for all because of all the moving we were doing. I am often reminded of how it can sneak up again, even though I believe I have mastered the problem. In this chapter, I will talk about my history with clutter and beyond that, how I changed up a few areas for the better such as my home décor and wardrobe. In the next chapter, I will share with you two areas in my home that I transformed, which made a big impact on my family.

My clutter past

Because I am a creative and visual person, I am inspired by things I see or read. Tons of magazine clippings, books, colorful handouts, endless crafting items, scrapbooking supplies, and party planning stuff make up most of my personal clutter. I also used to love buying new handbags and wallets and enjoyed working in the accessories department at Gottschalks Department Store when I was a teen. That is probably where my obsession started. Add to that, my creative clutter and all the photos and kids school stuff I saved through the years, and it became too much.

Since I am a writer and a party planner, a lot of things speak to me and even though I don't need the items at that moment, I want to be able to get my hands on them when I do. But there is only so much room for things in our lives and that is when it becomes a problem. This is something that has never overrun my life but certainly has been a thorn in my side through the years.

I tried so desperately to get a handle on my clutter tendencies, but nothing ever stuck. I remember writing a column in my junior college newspaper and one of my topics was the idea of being the most disorganized organized person I knew. I wrote about trying out a variety of organizing systems, having multiple to-do lists on several notepads, buying a variety of storage containers and baskets and reading every organizing book I could find and yet I still wasn't near as organized as I knew I could be. That article applied to me at 40 as much as it did when I wrote it at 20.

The funny thing is that I had no problem organizing other people's homes. In fact, I dabbled in professional organizing for a few years because I loved doing it so much. But when it came to my own home, I simply could not figure out how to let go of the clutter of previous years or how to manage the incoming papers and items that come in daily. Things that no longer fit in my new life seemed

to follow me whenever I moved, and I couldn't mentally or physically part with it.

I think the biggest headache for me was having too many boxes labeled MISC or TO SORT THRU stuffed in my bedroom closet, garage, hall corners and off-site storage unit. Just the mere site of those boxes would make me feel undisciplined, out of control and like a failure for not being able to solve this life-long problem. While some people are fine with having more clutter in their lives than others, for me it just makes the crowded thoughts in my brain go into overdrive when things are not in their place and my house looks in constant overflow.

Through the process of downsizing from a nearly 3,000 square foot home to a rented 1,600 square foot condo, to an even smaller rental at 900 square feet, followed by an extended stay in a hotel room my family and a puppy, I learned what things we truly needed daily. While difficult at the time, this process benefitted my family because by the time we moved into our smallish but cute permanent home, it felt at first like the Taj Mahal and it was ours!

A fresh style for my new life

In addition to overcoming my clutter problem, I had a chance to change my home décor style when we moved back to California. I continued to refine it with each following move. I went from saturated Tuscan colors of eggplant and red with big scale furnishings and chunky accessories in our large Arizona home to an uncluttered smaller Southern California home, with a modern and fresh feel. I chose gray, white and black colors with simple green, nature-inspired accessories. We bring out pops of color during each of the seasons. I love the versatility of this look, and this palette is what makes me happy and works for our family.

I was also inspired by the home of one of my favorite Food Network celebrity chef's Ina Garten of Barefoot Contessa. It is a style I like to call casual earthy elegance. Whatever home décor style you are drawn to, pick out what you like the best and let go of the rest. As the saying goes, your home should rise to meet you each day and a home that reflects your favorite items, values and interests is a beautiful and comfortable home. Be sure to make your surroundings match who you are today and not who you were years ago.

Streamlining my wardrobe

Another thing I did when I knew I had a major life transition ahead of me was to streamline my wardrobe. It was one of the best decisions I made, and I can't get over how easy it is for me to keep it going more than a decade later.

Especially with having two daughters, I never had a big budget for clothes, but I like to look nice. I found that I would often buy sale or clearance items that didn't match other items in my closet, or I wouldn't have the right accessories to go with it. I also knew I would have a much smaller closet than the large walk-in one I enjoyed in our Arizona home. In fact, my former closet in Arizona was larger than my entire kitchen in the home we have now. How I loved that closet!

Another thing that motivated me to narrow down my clothes colors was an inspiring 2010 *Good Housekeeping* article I read about actress and author Jamie Lee Curtis. She talked about streamlining her wardrobe and accessories to three main colors: navy, black and white. She admitted she wasn't much of a clothes horse but likes to look good and knew what looked best on her. Jamie Lee Curtis was right on the money because I did a similar thing, and it has served me well ever since.

I started one weekend by taking all my clothes, shoes and accessories out of my closet and anywhere in the house and garage and divided them into different color piles. After I thought about my favorite colors on me, I chose four neutral colors for basics and berry colors for the accents.

Unless I really loved something, if a clothing item or accessory (shoes, necklaces and scarves) didn't fall into one of those color piles, I gave it to charity or someone I knew who would like it.

Another tip Curtis shared in the article was to pretend you are packing for two trips, one during the winter and one in the summer. Look at all the clothes you plan to wear in two weeks and that will give you an idea of what the most wearable and favorite clothes are in your closet. Those clothes and shoes should be mostly what you keep for your base wardrobe.

For those who have had their colors done, I look best in a winter palette and my style is classic. So, the colors I chose were:

Neutral colors: navy, black, gray and white

Accessories: mostly silver and necklaces and scarves in solid colors as well as in combinations or patterns using some or all colors

Accent colors: different shades of berry such as magenta, lilac, eggplant and purple. I have also incorporated wearing red again year-round, and the color matches my neutral colors effortlessly.

My colors make up approximately 90% of what I have in my closet right now and the remaining items are other accent colors for a fun pop of color like vibrant yellow, tangerine and royal blue. This has helped me save money and time since I still shop the sales, but I can now go right to the items that are in my color palette and ignore the others. I literally wear most everything in my closet on a regular basis and am quick to give away clothes or shoes the

moment I no longer love wearing them or they are past their prime condition.

I rarely make shopping mistakes these days and I always can create a variety of different looks when I buy a new item in one of my chosen colors. It takes me no time at all to pick an outfit to wear on the fly and with my busy schedule that fact alone was so worth the effort to do it.

- ❖ Has a recent trauma or life-changing situation caused you to start or accelerate a hoarding problem in your life?

- ❖ Are there areas in your life you can streamline to make it easier for yourself like your wardrobe, kitchen or commitments?

- ❖ If you have been holding on to clutter and want to move forward and get rid of it, what do you think is holding you back from doing so? Explore your mental blocks and figure out how to work through them so you can tackle this task and feel lighter from less clutter. Get support from family and/or friends, paid laborers or a professional organizer to help you get rid of your clutter.

- ❖ What are some of your most precious items that you can make space for after you give away the excess clutter of items that no longer have value to you?

CHAPTER SIX

Prevent Clutter from Becoming Invasive

Clutter is a physical manifestation of fear that cripples our

ability to grow

---H. G. Chissell

Just because you go through mounds of clutter and get your problems areas uncluttered, that doesn't mean the problem is solved. Unless you have systems in place that work for you and your family, the clutter will continue to be a problem, just like weeds are to a garden.

When you choose to have minimal clutter and pick it up as you go, it is like pulling small weak weeds out of your garden on a regular basis. However, if you let clutter control you, it is like massive monster weeds that are deep in the ground and take multiple hours to remove.

I chose to make it easier on myself and minimize the constant clutter that comes in my life, so it no longer controls me and causes me shame. What a difference it has made. The two organizing systems I put in place that had the most positive impact were my home command central and garage.

Home command center

I did not completely master this problem area until recently about a year or two after we moved into our newest home in Southern California. I tried many different systems but none of them worked for very long and I always felt frustrated and unorganized. What typically would happen is "stuff" would pile up and be left all around the house. Then when company was coming over, I would frantically scoop them up and dump them into a large storage box and slap a MISC label on it. I would then put it in a closet or the garage until I desperately needed something from it, and I would go through the box.

Here is what finally worked for me and if this is a problem for you too, I hope it can inspire you to set up your own system that helps you manage the everyday stuff that comes into your life. This can be set up for any size family, people who have partners or roommates or a busy single person. I listed below each of the different categories of our "stuff" and where we keep it.

- **Keys, glasses, wallets, etc.**

- o I have a basket near my front door that has a place for keys and small items.

- **Current reading materials**

  - o A decorative basket in my front room contains magazines and books I am reading. I have a nearby container on my coffee table that holds my reading glasses and highlighter pens.

- **Incoming mail to sort through**

  - o We keep a decorative basket on the kitchen counter that is big enough to hold a week's worth of mail to go through on the weekend.

- **Papers for upcoming events—tickets, clippings, invites**

  - o On a wall near the kitchen, I hang a wall organizer for all important papers that are needed soon

- **Master calendar**

  - o Located in a prominent position in kitchen for all to use

The rest of the items now go into a converted hall closet off my kitchen and this has been a lifesaver. It is functional and with a small house, everyday clutter piles up rather quickly and I needed a spot to corral these items into one place. I took off the door, painted the inside walls a darker shade of gray from the light gray in the rest of my home and added hooks to hang up purses and backpacks.

There is not a lot of room for coats and bulky sweaters, so I put those in each family member's closet, and it works for us since we have rather mild weather most months in Southern California. Here is what my home command closet holds for me:

- Four-tier floor rack for shoes

- Place to file current receipts. New checks.

- In a nearby kitchen drawer, I have office supplies—stapler, tape, writing utensils, pads of paper, post-it pads. I keep a few most used items in a thin hanging shelf organizer in the closet like AA batteries, tape, glue stick, hammer, envelopes, stamps and return labels.

Garage

The other big clutter hot spot for me is the garage and for years it served as a place of shame for my husband and I because we could never control the clutter. It was difficult to get rid of things that still looked good, and I thought I could use it someday for a craft project, theme party, costume—you name it and I had an excuse for keeping it.

I can't tell you how painful it was to be forced to go through items in a storage unit or two and garage and try to get through it without feeling bad. I felt sick to my stomach when I would think of the money or time wasted keeping that item, but then I would make the mistake of thinking that by keeping it somehow, I would get the value back. No such luck and when I finally realized that it made it so much easier to go through each item and either throw it away or give it away if I couldn't see it fitting it my new life.

Inspired by organizer Marie Kondo, I am now saying a quick thank you for each item, regardless of the value it had in my life, because obviously at one time I believed it did have value, otherwise I would not have held onto it.

Quite often, items I had been keeping in storage for years no longer had value (whether that value was spent wisely or wasted, didn't matter) so why not pass it along to someone else who could get full value from it instead of it wasting away in my garage or storage unit? This concept applied to an unread book as well as a piece of furniture that didn't match my new décor style.

We haven't paid for a storage unit since 2017 and saving $220 a month (which rose every year) has really benefitted our family. Using a storage unit was a good option when we needed it, but if you have one or more units and they are not serving a higher purpose for you, I recommend going through your clutter and moving it on. Just think about the savings you can enjoy by not paying for off-site storage.

One of the few exceptions was saving useful or beautiful containers or baskets, which I use to hold other items of value to me or to put homemade goodies or gift items for others. The de-cluttering process started getting easier once I changed the way I thought about my clutter.

Here is the process that helped, and I hope it can help you if a cluttered storage unit and/or garage is something you struggle with.

1. **Make a list of all the different categories your "stuff" falls into.**

   Here is a partial list of my clutter categories:

   - Craft and gift supplies

   - Home repair, maintenance, tools, painting supplies

   - Cleaning supplies, rags, outdoor towels

   - Entertaining and party theme items

   - Scrapbooks, photos, albums, kids' memorabilia

   - Containers and boxes of all types

   - Picnic items—blankets, fold-away tables and chairs

   - Sports items—tennis racquets, bikes, surfboards

2. To deal with my many storage boxes containing a mish mosh of items or piles in areas of my garage, I emptied each one and **put them all into one massive pile as big as I had time to sort through that day.**

3. **Before I started sorting, I would have large empty boxes marked with my different categories and one for trash and one for charity.** I loved the idea I saw on an organizing show that you go "shopping" through your stuff and only take what will fit into your life as it is NOW.

For example, I realized that unless I was starting a party planning business, I no longer needed the plastic pink flamingos packed away for that one day I would have a request to throw a pink flamingo-themed party.

I basically thought about the main party themes I like to plan and kept most of those items and gave away the rest to charity. Each theme had its own storage box, which includes relevant music CD's, themed serving dishes, paper goods, decorations and magazine articles about the theme. My themes include Mexican, Greek, French and nautical.

4. **If an item wasn't in good condition, I didn't think twice to put it in the trash.** No one wants your icky, damaged and smelly items even if you think someone can wash it, repair it or fix it. The only exception I made were items someone could paint and make better or use for their outdoor areas. Anything short of that, I got rid of it. For example, why was I holding onto mounds of paper and stationery, which was half damaged, when it could just go in the recycle bin?

5. **Once I went through the big pile and shopped my way through my clutter, whatever was left over from the pile was thrown away.** If you spend too much time thinking about it, it will probably end up getting stuffed in another box only to get packed away in your garage or unit to be dealt with another day. Who has time for that?

6. **Last, take everything that is left over and put similar things together.** Whether the items went in my house, garage or storage unit, I always try to keep like items together. For example, in my garage, I sectioned off areas into different zones as professional organizer Julie Morgenstern recommends in her fantastic book, *Organizing from Within*. She recommends setting up areas like a kindergarten class where everything has its own zones.

   Here are some of the zones I set up in my garage:

   - Laundry and folding zone
   - Gift-wrapping supplies (now in spare room)
   - Labeled boxes that contain party themes
   - Storage cabinet for all home repair supplies such as tools, painting and maintenance
   - Large shelf for entertaining items and overflow from kitchen
   - Travel items on big shelf – luggage, smaller bags, backpacks

- Sport items zone
- Outdoor activities shelf for large beach towels, fold-up picnic tables and blankets, coolers and containers
- Sleepover items like comforters, pillows and sleeping bags
- Holiday and seasonal storage boxes

Strategies for everyday clutter

Discard paper and trash as soon as possible. We make faster decisions now on what belongs in our house so if it doesn't, it goes in trash or recycle bin as soon as possible. I have to say that this habit has made a huge difference for me in keeping my home cleaner and more organized. We also throw any trash away that is in the car while getting gas and when leaving the car at the end of the day.

When I get the mail, I clip out what I need to look at later or coupons I use (putting them in the coupon bin) and recycle the rest. I have my girls empty out trash cans around the house every few days as much as we can.

Gather all glasses, dishes and utensils by the end of day around the house and put them in dishwasher or rinsed and in sink if busy. Before my kids got older and were gone working part-time jobs, they were responsible for keeping dishwasher emptied daily so we could always run the dishwasher one or two times a day if needed.

We use our home command closet daily and keep all important items there and misc. items like shoes and backpacks. This has helped us tremendously to keep things in one area.

After a day trip or longer, put things in clothes washer and other items away as soon as possible. We empty all our luggage and bags as soon as we get home and put things either in the wash or in the rooms they belong to and put bags away. The same applies to sleepovers so we can see if something is missing, and we need to make calls to follow up on lost items.

Allow time to put things away after an event at the house. After any event, by the next day, we wash all the serving dishes and put them away along with any theme items or special items into their appropriate storage boxes. My goal is for the house and car to look as tidy as they were before the event and believe me that was never the case years before.

Teach family members how to do their own laundry. This has been a tremendous help, and kids can help with washing towels and sheets, trash duty, meal making, emptying dishwasher and wherever else you need a helping hand. I honestly can't believe how much calmer I am as a working mother when my girls pitched in more around the house.

Do bite-size organizing projects when you don't have a big chunk of time available. It's amazing what you can do in 10 or 15 minutes that can make a difference in your daily routine. Mini projects can include straightening up the linen closet or under the sink cabinets or your makeup drawer. I go through my closets whenever I can and take out clothes for charity and have my girls do the same. By keeping up on this, I don't have to devote hours upon hours on de-cluttering projects.

Questions to ask yourself:

❖ What is your personal and family clutter?

❖ How do you handle the everyday clutter that comes into your life each day?

❖ Are you happy with your closet and your wardrobe? If you could only keep three neutral colors and three accent colors, what would they be? Have you ever had your colors done—what season are you? What colors make you feel happy when you wear them?

❖ How do you keep the clutter of your past from creeping into your present and future?

CHAPTER SEVEN

Cultivate a Child-like Spirit

Let your life lightly dance on the edges of time like dew on the tip of a leaf

--Rabindranath Tagore

As I started working on this chapter, I saw a scene from a movie on television later that day that drove home the point I wanted to make. It was the 2004 movie, *Raising Helen,* starring Kate Hudson and Joan Cusack. Hudson played the role of Helen, a Manhattan fashion executive who becomes the guardian of her sister's three children after her sister and husband die in a tragic car accident.

After having a tough time with the feelings of loss and the many changes in all their lives (like moving to a new community and schools), a friend suggests to Helen to take the kids for some play time at the zoo.

Having fun outside in nature with the animals was exactly what they all needed and helped to lighten the heaviness of their difficult situation.

Playing through the stress

When my girls and I joined my husband in California that first summer after our girls finished school in Arizona, we moved into a very small, old and less-than-pleasant condo, while we looked for a home to purchase. The girls missed their friends and dogs terribly and were not used to California yet. Everything felt unfamiliar and uncomfortable. It was also stressful looking for a home and all that goes with that and every home for sale seemed to be either a complicated short sale or out of our budget.

What really helped lighten the mood for us were all the little things we did that made us feel like kids on summer vacation. We rode our bikes together (something we couldn't do in July in Phoenix) and spent time at the lake across the street. One Saturday we made a trip to the American Girl Store at the Grove Shopping Center in Los Angeles and immersed ourselves in the world of dolls then drove down Pacific Coast Highway all the way home.

Another weekend we went to beach festival San Diego with my sister Michelle and niece Madelyn, and we celebrated my brother-in-law Doug's birthday another weekend in San Diego listening to jazz music at a cigar bar with their group of friends.

We had a fun time at the end of July watching the dachshund race at Old World Village in Huntington Beach and another time we went sailing on a friend's boat in Newport. We also met up with family in Huntington Beach during the U.S. Open Surf week. Another time was spent with friends from our past and we thoroughly enjoyed catching up with them and meeting their friends and family. We also enjoyed the times when out-of-town loved ones came to visit us.

All these little excursions and meet-ups were significant in keeping us focused on the present and not on the tough time we were having trying to find a home and secure the girls in the right schools. Everything else seemed like so much effort and the days when we were out "playing" made us feel alive and happy and thankful for our family.

A garden for joy

Flash forward six months later and after a long and painful escrow process, moving two more times and my husband being near death over Christmas weekend, I ended up in a depressive state as I discussed earlier. However, one of the things that helped me to move through that difficult time and find joy again was rediscovering my love of gardening. It was something I couldn't do much while I lived in Phoenix. In contrast, my California home had sunny mild weather, rich soil and lots of room to plant things.

I was introduced to the hobby of gardening shortly after I remarried. My husband's mom was and still is a talented gardener and the gardens she created and tended to in the front and back of her Bay Area home should have been featured in Sunset Magazine as they were stunning. Although I always loved the idea of gardening, let's just say I didn't take to it like a duck to water.

I remember the spring after we were married, I spent a long Saturday cleaning up the garden in our OC home that was started by the previous owners and the flowers were planted in a haphazard way around our yard. At the end of the day, I remember sitting in a mound of mud feeling dirty and exhausted and looking like I had been run over by a tractor. I said to my husband, *"I really don't get the appeal of this!"* He laughed and said *"Well, try again next season and see what you think."*

It was partly because I didn't have the experience of knowing what I was doing. He was right because sure enough by summer, I got the hang of it and have enjoyed gardening ever since. If you had told me on that first day of gardening that someday I would write a book with a gardening theme, I would have thought you were pulling my leg!

Now when I am gardening, it is as close to feeling like a child as it gets, and I love it. I am in my play clothes, hands in dirt, worms crawling around me and I have colorful flowers to create, just as a child uses crayons to draw. The process of gardening and enjoying the results feels magical to me.

It is a bit ironic about my desire to feel like a child at times because most of my childhood, I wanted to be a grown up. As far back as I can remember, I couldn't wait to be an adult and would prefer to participate in my mom's conversations with the neighbors or my aunts rather than kids my own age.

That was me – a crazy 15-year-old girl who liked watching business shows and *Meet the Press* every Sunday morning (and still do). I bought her first hunter green "power" suit at age 16. I was like a female version of Alex P. Keaton in the popular 80s sitcom *Family Ties,* played by the talented Michael J. Fox. It's funny how we evolve. Having children has certainly brought out the inner child deep within me but you don't need kids to do that.

Participate in activities just for the fun of it

Especially after becoming a mom, I've struggled with taking the time to pursue activities that make me feel completely in the moment as a child does. I have always worked on creative projects, but it was usually for someone else or an event. Even when I baked, which I love to do, it was always for a goal in mind like the holidays or someone's birthday or school event. What I'm referring to are activities that you do just for you and for the joy of it.

An example is someone who engages in a sport just for fun such as swimming, tennis or paddle boarding. Or another person might read a book just for the pleasure of it while sitting under a tree at a local park or the beach to completely get away from it all. Other activities that cultivate a child-like spirit include dancing, roller skating, bowling, riding bumper cars, horseback riding, sailing, or taking classes such as pottery, art, cooking or cake decorating.

Some other fun activities include playing board games, visiting a museum or science center or any place to learn something new like for us visiting the Ocean Institute in Dana Point or going on a whale watching cruise. How about attending a county fair and learning more about the animals, finding out how ice cream is made or visiting a farmer's market and talking to the growers? The choices are endless

The key is finding activities that put you in the state of flow, a term coined by Mihaly Csikszentmihalyi, author of the book *Flow*. It is when you are involved in an activity that nothing seems to matter, and you just get lost in time much like the earlier quote about dancing at the edge of time like dew on the tip of a leaf.

When in the flow, time melts away and all that is left is the pure joy of the activity itself.

Add spontaneity back in your Life

Another aspect of having a child-like spirit that can help during a difficult time is allowing for a little spontaneity in your life. One of the most spontaneous things we did during our transitional and difficult time was adopting a puppy we saw at the mall. Having a puppy in the middle of everything was a challenge, but our little, loving Cooper kept us in the present and gave us so much joy - even when he could sometimes be a little stinker like any puppy can.

Another spontaneous thing I did after I was starting to feel a lot better in the beginning of 2013 was to look for a local group of people to play tennis with. I found one through Meetup.com. I hadn't really thought about it but one day it just sounded good, and I went to play tennis that night after I first signed up. I really enjoyed my time with my new tennis friends and if I had given it too much thought that day then I probably would have talked myself out of it.

Being spontaneous can be as simple as accepting a last-minute invitation to go somewhere with a friend or someone you would like to get to know better or doing something you hadn't planned on that could potentially bring you joy for doing it. Now for some of you, spontaneity may come easily but for me, the Virgo planner girl, it was not an easy trait to develop but I know now it has helped me to be happier overall.

The power of nappy time

For most of you, you probably remember when you were in kindergarten and after lunch, you and your classmates took a little nap. You would typically lie on your little mat with the lights low and soothing music in the background for a little while before you started learning again? Doesn't that bring a smile to your face?

As adults, we tend to discount the power of time out or a delicious nap, and that is unfortunate. Taking a break gives your mind a mental break to just let it empty out and rest from all the sights and sounds, worries and stresses that can wear us out if we don't recharge during the day. For some, it is called meditation and for others it is a nap.

Getting enough sleep and allowing yourself time to let your brain rest during the day is not just for ordinary folk. The movers of shakers of the world have also learned the importance of taking breaks and getting enough sleep to have the energy to get through the day.

In her book *Thrive: The Third Metric to Redefining Success and Creating a Life of Well-Being, Wisdom and Wonder,* author Arianna Huffington (founder of the Huffington Post) discusses how she burned out on the job after working 18 hours days and how important it was for her to take proper care of herself and not think of work 24/7.

After collapsing from exhaustion one day and hurting herself from falling to the ground, she knew something had to change. She mentioned in an interview with Oprah on Super Soul Sunday in 2014 that she now gets plenty of rest each night and removes all electronics from her bedroom before she retires at the end of her day. I like that idea and would add to disconnect from technology for a bit during your day (and I mean phones too) and take that needed adult "quiet time" whether you choose to nap or not.

When things are especially stressful or I am struggling to get enough sleep in, I try to have a 20-minute nap around noon time. Afterward I always feel sharper and more energetic for my afternoon tasks. That one activity gives me the energy to get through the rest of my workday, long commute and family and home obligations after I get home from work.

When you are stuck in the muck after tragedy or a very difficult time, your mind is probably racing or stuck in a negative cycle and I know for me, I was constantly going through in my mind too many negative thoughts of the past, present and future. It was a lot of noise that exhausted me emotionally as well as physically. What the power of nappy time did for me was to give my mind a rest from everything—the worry, speculation, regretful thinking etc. so I could power myself up to do something fun or productive.

Think of adult nappy or quiet time as a beautiful and necessary thing to plan in your day. You deserve to give yourself the time you need each night to get the sleep your individual body needs to feel refreshed and productive in the morning.

Questions to ask yourself

- Is there an activity that you do that makes you feel alive and youthful? Is there something that puts you in the "flow" and gives you energy after you do it and you feel you could do for hours at a time?

- Have you thought of revisiting a childhood passion and starting it up again?

- Is there a regular time during the day that you can schedule your adult "nappy" or quiet time and disconnect from the world and recharge yourself?

CHAPTER EIGHT

Nurture Positive Connections

Let us be grateful to the people who make us happy.

They are the charming gardeners who make our souls blossom

--Marcel Proust

Gratitude is the word that comes to mind when I think of the people who have touched my soul through the years with their love and friendship. I concur completely with the numerous studies I read that say having strong connections and feeling loved by others is a key ingredient to a happy life. It also plays a role in being healthier, living longer and having more resilience when times get rough.

A flower cannot blossom without sunshine, and man cannot live without love.
-Max Miller

Going through my difficult two-and-a-half year period and at times feeling in the darkest of places, I truly believe that if it wasn't for feeling loved by the people in my life or at the very least having some form of face-to-face connection with someone during the day, I don't know how it would have ended up for me on my darkest of dark days.

To say that love saved my life sounds so cliché but, in my case, it is the truth. My connections with people truly moved me from a place of desperation to inspiration.

Some days the pace of the world felt like it was going too fast for me, and I remember feeling like a rag spinning inside a dryer. Or other days I felt the opposite, so slow that every inch of my body was weighed down with sadness. But it was usually the sound of a loved one's voice or a simple hug that would remind me that I was loved, and this feeling too shall pass.

On one of those especially bad days, I remember feeling so epically overwhelmed by my work, the kids and a messy house that I was sobbing terribly and could not stop. Believe it or not, what snapped me out of it was a kind and chatty handyman in his late 50's, who was scheduled to come by in the morning to install my dishwasher. He had a gentle yet scruffy look about him and reminded me of the lead TV character Columbo of the *Columbo* series in the 1970s played by the late Peter Falk.

We instantly bonded like we had known each other for years and had an hour-plus conversation as he worked in my kitchen. He shared with me the troubles he was having with a granddaughter he never gets to see and an adult child who is in and out of trouble and the many hours he works and the long commute he must endure each day.

I was moved when he shared with me that no matter what was going on in his life, he always found good in every situation and had gratitude every single day. He then listened to me as I told him about what I had been through and the stressful day I was having, since he could clearly see I had been crying with my red puffy face. After our connection and conversation, I felt a ton better.

Our interaction was so simple yet powerful for me that when he left, I felt like he was an angel sent down from heaven at just the right time to help pull me out of a downward spiral. Now that I am better, I look for opportunities where I can be that angel to someone else struggling like I was.

I couldn't possibly talk any further about positive connections in this chapter without mentioning my friend Sue, who passed away in 2011, and who I dedicated this book to. I am sure if you asked any family member or close friend of hers that they would agree that Sue was the gold standard when it came to giving love with your whole heart and making time to connect with family and close friends. As one of her dear friends Erin said at her Celebration of Life event held at Saddleback Church, *if you knew Sue then you knew what it was like to be truly loved.*

For me, I will never forget the way her face would light up whenever we got together or how we would spend a girls' weekend together with another close friend and before we finished that weekend, she was planning for the next time to get together. Sue's wholehearted loving spirit touched so many people and we are all better for knowing her.

Even when life is going well, it is a challenge to regularly connect with people we care about but throw in tough times, and it can make it downright impossible. I think it is because we are so overwhelmed with the chaos in our lives and the fact that we don't want to burden others with our troubles. It's easy for us to isolate ourselves because we think that no one else would understand. I believe there could be nothing farther from the truth.

I experienced it firsthand in my own life. Looking back over my difficult period, I clearly can see that when I didn't regularly engage with others is when I felt the worst. We moved out of our home in late fall 2010 and the girls and I moved into a condo down the street to finish the girls' school year before joining my husband later that summer in California. I started to isolate myself a bit around that time, but by early February 2011 after my friend Sue had passed away suddenly, I spent most days holed up in my condo, immersed in sadness.

The warmth of a friend's presence brings joy to our hearts, sunlight to our souls, and pleasure to all of life.

--author unknown

What brought light to my dreary colorless days that spring (the fact that in my mind they were dreary, and I lived in Phoenix says a lot) was when people from out of town came to visit us like my sister, aunt and cousin and my parents when my younger daughter celebrated a big milestone at church. Of course, I enjoyed it when my husband came home once a month, but his visits were brief, and our talks were mainly about the kids and moving logistics. That and regular chats with a few close girlfriends and saying hi and bye to parents of my girls' friends, was the extent of my connecting with others.

When depression hit me again the same season one year later, it was again my connection with loved ones that brought me back into the light. Events like my parent's anniversary party and husband's milestone birthday event was like a joy fest for me because I was surrounded by my parents, aunts, cousins, longtime friends and other family members who made me feel connected and loved me just for me.

Later that fall, I planned a girls' weekend away in the Bay Area with my extended family and they hosted two different gathering events when I came into town, which meant so much to me. I also spent quality time in November with my girlfriend and family in Arizona and that was wonderful.

By the time the holidays of 2012 rolled around, my emotional well was no longer empty, and I felt truly over my sadness and depression. It was nearly overflowing by the time I hosted Christmas dinner at my house for my parents, sister and her family. I honestly felt the best I had in 2 ½ years.

I have read countless books and studies on happiness, longevity and having resilience and I can say nearly 95 percent of my readings include the importance of having authentic connections with others. I believe so strongly in this research that I have made it a side passion to communicate this important research through my blog (www.livinghappilyconnected.com), writing books and articles and speaking on occasion to encourage people to stay connected and make more positive connections in their lives.

Seeking support during the tough times

Whether you are in crisis or in recovery mode, it is important to not isolate yourself and try to do it all on your own. As I mentioned in the previous chapter about shame, Brené Brown's research proved that we are hard wired for connection—our mind, body and soul need it just as we need oxygen to breathe. There are different types of people you can reach out to, but the point is to reach out to someone. Here are some suggestions:

Family members usually come first to mind. You may have a strained relationship with a family member and unless it is especially toxic (I will discuss that in a bit), reaching out to them to get some emotional support, even if it is limited, is better than no connection at all.

Time spent with a **supportive spouse, best friend or close friend** can also give you the emotional support you need. Make sure the person is trustworthy and has your back and will keep things between the two of you. Trust is an important part of a close friendship because the last thing you need is someone who will take your confidence and blab it to others or to judge you or to throw it back in your face at another time.

Other places where you can connect and get emotional support can be from church. For example, if you are a member of a **small group at church,** do not hesitate to bring them in to give you support. Pastor Rick Warren of Saddleback Church shared with his congregation that the day his son passed. He was out on the driveway with his wife Kay, every one of his small group members were at his house within minutes to give him a hug and grieve with him. *"They didn't have to say a word, but their presence meant everything to me,"* Warren shared.

Caring neighbors or parents of your children's friends can also be a big help during times of stress. I remember when my youngest was a baby, I went back to work while my husband went back to school for a year (watching our baby during the day) and I was suffering for a brief time from postpartum depression. I remember one morning when I was leaving the house full of tears and my friend and neighbor Kerri was driving by my house on the way to work and could see my sad and crying face. She pulled over, got out of her car and gave me a big hug and assured me that everything was going to be ok. That little gesture meant the world to me and was exactly what I needed at the time.

Or another time I was especially moved when three new moms I met (Dana, Seema and Karen) when I first moved to Orange County and brought over full home-cooked meals for my family to enjoy after my husband came home from almost dying in the hospital. Yes, their food was delicious, and our tummies were full, but it was their kind gestures that truly warmed our souls the most. It made us thankful for having such thoughtful friends in our lives. Be open to kind gestures from people around you and don't be afraid to ask for help when you need it. When someone asks to pick up a few groceries when you are sick, let them or if they ask if they can help, tell them what you need. Then return the favor and pay it forward when you are in the position to do so.

Another time about three weeks before Christmas 2013, my husband's job was eliminated with no warning, and it threw me into an emotional time once again. Uncomfortable feelings of uncertainty and fear found their way back into my head. His layoff seemed to kick off a series of other sad and difficult challenges including my daughter's health, finding out my good friend Marilyn's husband had died (they were together more than 60 years), and home issues started to pop up. We kept the news from our girls until January and only let a few people know what we were going through since it was the holiday season after all.

I had noticed that my neighbor's husband had been home a lot in December like my husband, and while I didn't know he and his wife well (they had moved into the neighborhood about five months prior during a busy time for us), his wife seemed a little sad when I would see her occasionally. A few days after Christmas when I was especially feeling overwhelmed, I saw her outside and asked her how *she* was doing. She started to cry and told me that her husband had lost his job early in December. Ironically, it was the same day my hubby lost his. We bonded over that and talked daily about our worries and how we could stay positive for our husbands. We leaned on each other for support. I can't tell you how much being a support to her helped me feel better too. Later, not only did our husbands lose their jobs on the same day, but they also both started their new jobs on the same day. What are the odds of that?

I still had my circle of friends and family who helped me through another challenging time but having someone to lean on in person and hug on a regular basis and chat face-to-face on her porch was a wonderful gift.

There is nothing that can replace a hug, an understanding look or sharing tears or laughter with someone in person who really knows and loves you.

Make time for face-to-face connecting

My neighbor's story is an example of the importance of spending time with people face-to-face. I know we live in a different day and age where people stay connected through social media like Facebook and Instagram and believe me, I do it too. But in my opinion, that is only one-dimensional connecting. Especially during the rough times, there is nothing that can replace a hug, a look of understanding or the bond of sharing tears or laughter with someone in person who really knows and loves you. I really saw the power of that in the prior examples I just gave.

In happiness research conducted by Dan Buettner, he discovered that having strong social bonds and being a member of a close-knit community of people can make it possible for someone who has just enough money and a modest life to be *happier* than someone who has a lot of material wealth and possessions but feels no real connection with others. Buettner is a former *National Geographic* researcher and founder of the Blue Zones, areas with the most centenarians.

What sunshine is to flowers, smiles are to humanity. These are but trifles, to be sure; but scattered along life's pathway, the good they do is inconceivable.

-Joseph Addison

Another study I read from Buettner stated that toll booth operators rank high on the list of jobs that have the happiest workers, and you know why? Because they spend at least five hours each day interacting with people face to face even for only a few minutes at a time. Just think about how you feel when you get a big smile from the toll booth person or someone handing you your morning coffee or fast-food meal in the drive thru line? Doesn't it make you perk up a little versus someone being grouchy and frowning at you? If everyone gave smiles at one

another, I think those good feelings would spread and I bet the world would be a nicer place to live in.

I had a falling out with my best girlfriend years ago partially because of our lack of face-to-face connection. This was someone I talked to on the phone four or more times a week and sometimes even a few times a day. However, when it came to face-to-face connection, I saw her only once every seven or eight years.

For years when we would schedule times to meet (first we lived five hours away from each other and then in different states), she would always find an excuse to cancel. When we were in the process of moving back to California, and things were starting to feel strained with us on the phone. I felt like I was being fully open with her, but she was holding back.

The distance and lack of face-to-face connection was feeling like a wedge growing between us, which was hard for me because she was my closest confidant. While I was 100 percent honest with her on the good and bad things going on in my life, I found out that she was hiding the negative things going on in her life and had been for years. I believe best friends need to be real and authentic with each other otherwise why be best friends?

Right before my family and I went through the escrow from hell in the fall of 2011, I confronted my friend about something and told her that I thought she wasn't being honest with me. Less than 10 minutes into the conversation, she said she couldn't deal with it and got off the phone abruptly. Within an hour, she not only "un-friended" me on Facebook but blocked me so I could never send her a message on social media. She also didn't answer my texts, and I never heard from her again. No call, no text, no email or letter…nothing.

That was more than a decade ago now and this was someone who I had known since high school – who was my best friend for two decades and honorary Godmother to my second daughter. How easy it seemed for her to hang up and erase me from her life when she didn't have to look me in the eye to tell me how she was feeling. That is the problem with not seeing someone face to face.

But with that said, I believe that some friendships do have expiration dates and if someone close to you doesn't fit into your new life after a big transition or crisis you have gone through, there is no need for a big blow up. For example, weeks before my falling out with my friend, I was getting a weird vibe from her, and I couldn't put my finger on it. Our differences seemed to outweigh what we had in common and when I was direct that day and broached a sensitive subject, it was clear that our relationship couldn't hold up to that kind of honesty. While that would have been ok for someone you only see occasionally, that didn't work for someone who I considered my best friend.

The lesson I learned is that sometimes it is best to move on and wish the person well and not include them in your new life when the relationship doesn't fit your life anymore. After I got over the hurt of losing her, I was glad that our friendship ended abruptly as it did - like a bandage ripped from my skin. Without a big argument and bad things said to each other, it allowed me to focus on the good things about our friendship and she will always have a special place in my heart.

Pull out the suckers

When I first started gardening, my mother-in-law was over visiting from Oregon and gave me some pointers on how to grow a beautiful and tidy garden. One of the things she taught me was to look for "suckers", underground plant runners usually found under trees, shrubs or other plants that suck away all the nutrients and water from the healthy plants and flowers.

If you don't pull them out, they can grow to be as big as a regular plant and invade your healthy garden.

Just like plant suckers, people "suckers" drain you of your time, energy and positive outlook and invade the healthy garden of your soul. Since my 20's, I have been lucky to have only one girlfriend "sucker" in my life at a time but now that I know what I know, I am aiming for none at a time and while not easy, it seems to be going well so far.

In Dr. Phil's book *Life Code*, he discusses having these types of people in your life. For purposes of this book and in my own experience and research, you should be aware that when in crisis or in recovery, a people sucker will do one or more of the following (see next page) so look out for this type of person:

- Makes you feel bad, judging you about the decisions you've made
- Makes you feel like you somehow deserve or brought on bad things happening to you
- Asks for feedback on how he or she has hurt you and when you tell them, they turn it on you and make it about *you* hurting *them*
- Shines a spotlight on your weaknesses and puts down your efforts to reinvent yourself or make positive changes in your life
- After spending time with them, you feel worse instead of better

If you have one or more of these people in your life, consider minimizing the relationship and time you spend with them. Or if the person is causing you constant grief, you may want to pull them out of your life completely.

Doing for others can be the best medicine

Friendship can weather most things and thrive in thin soil - but it needs a little mulch of letters and phone calls and small silly presents every so often just to save it from drying out completely.

- Pam Brown

There are many studies that prove that when we do for others, we feel better about ourselves, so take the time to nurture the good relationships you have in your life. Phone calls, sending little cards and gifts to thank people who have been there for you, forwarding silly notes through email or regular texts is like adding fertilizer to your relationship garden.

Lifestyle author Alexandra Stoddard talks about these little gestures of love, which she calls *ninis,* in her books and keeps a stock of her own small thoughtful gifts to send out to beloved family and friends to let them know she is thinking of them.

When you give to others, whether a small gift of friendship or offering to help someone in need or anything in between, it can help take the emphasis off your own problems for a while and says to your mind that you must not be as bad as you think because you are able to give to someone else.

Of course, this is after the worst of your situation has passed, but in some cases, helping others can help bring you out of your negative situation faster emotionally. At the very least, it can give you a reprieve from sadness, frustration or anger and give you something positive to focus on.

For example, a few weeks before my ex-husband and I decided to separate, I had signed up to participate in a local Working Wardrobes event to help battered women in shelters and I was to assist the attendees with writing their resumes. It turned out that the event was the day after my ex and I decided to separate, and although I wasn't feeling much in the mood to interact with others, I went anyway.

It felt good to talk with each lady about her hopes and dreams while helping with her resume, and I related to each of them starting a new chapter of their lives. It was one of the best eight hours I have ever spent in a day and put my divorce into perspective.

Questions to ask:

- ❖ Who are the people in your life who bring you the most joy and make you feel better after a conversation with them? Are you planning regular times to connect with them?
- ❖ Do you have others who do the opposite? How can you minimize time with those people?
- ❖ Overall, do you make enough time to spend with your family and friends who you love?

CHAPTER NINE

Celebrate That You are Like No Other

Don't wish to be normal. Wish to be yourself. To the hilt. Find out what you're best at and develop it and hopscotch your weaknesses. Wish to be great at whatever you are.

--Lois McMaster Bujold Labyrinth

I hope you have saved reading this chapter for last, because it really is the culmination of all the chapters before it. For me, once I created a new vision for myself, went at my own pace, got rid of shame, laughed more, felt good starting new things, removed clutter and embraced my inner child, I felt like I could truly embrace the new version of me and connect better with others. Not the victim version of me, but the survivor version of me.

This is the stage when I moved from surviving to thriving. My husband and I made the conscious decision to no longer identify as the couple who had all these difficult things happen to them, but instead is a close-knit family who, because of their struggles, is now stronger, happier, and more resilient than ever before.

If we say it long enough, eventually we are going to reap a harvest. We're going to get exactly what we are saying to ourselves

-Joel Osteen

Like Pastor Osteen says, we are who we say we are. When January 2013 rolled around, I was ready to reinvent myself and attacked my new side passion with gusto. I earned a certificate in Happiness Perspectives in January, created and launched my new blog in March, started playing tennis again in April and found a great local networking group to participate in by May.

By June, I co-hosted a local happiness workshop with a wellness client. And when my writing work slowed down over the summer, I brushed off the book notes I had planned to write and finished most of this book by my milestone birthday.

However, with that said, I've had my challenges in moving forward and it usually is because of the fear-based thoughts that find themselves back in my head. It's easy to allow those doubts to creep back in and tell you to not venture past your comfort zone or to not move forward when you don't have everything figured out. Or as a mom, when there is craziness at home, (as it often is with kids) that somehow you don't deserve to carve out something just for yourself.

But I have learned to work past those negative thoughts and be more fearless as I go after my dreams. I can do it utilizing my strengths while minimizing my weaknesses and being uniquely me. There is no more room for perfection in the new life garden I am creating for myself.

Embracing what is uniquely you

If you are ready to move forward and reinvent yourself or just start anew after surviving a tough time, the place to start is with YOU. If someone asked you what your personal brand is, what would you say? When I ask my girls, I love to hear them say what makes them special, what their interests are and what their current personal brand is. It is fun to hear how it changes a bit from year to year based on their interests at the time.

The best advice I can give to others wanting to bloom again and flourish after a big downpour in their life is to embrace what makes them unique. For example, for years I allowed a few close people I knew to define me as an emotional and sensitive person in negative terms like it was a weakness. Then one day I remember my close girlfriend Val saying to me, *"Cher, don't ever view your emotion as negative, because you feel with your whole heart and are a sensitive soul. We need more people like you in this world."*

That was the first time I truly looked at being emotional and sensitive in a positive way, and years later I now know there is a name for people like me. Psychiatrist and author Dr. Judith Orloff call these people "empaths". Both my older daughter and I are empaths and are using it to help others through our special gift. I hope to write more about this topic in future projects.

I realized that it helps me as a writer to be empathetic to others and it is a definite asset as I write blog articles about being connected to others. When asked in a personal branding workshop I attended in 2004, if I were to pick a company that best describes me, I said Hallmark because it embodies the values that are important to me, like helping people stay connected with one another and showing their love and appreciation through giving cards and gifts. A decade later, I created a blog that has similar values - funny how that works!

Every person is a combination of positive and negative traits and interesting backgrounds – all with a unique story to share. That is why I especially love writing bios for clients because I enjoy telling people's stories and bringing out what is special about them. After the dust settles from your difficult situation, how can your experiences add to your personal brand?

For example, I have a longtime friend who endured physical abuse in her childhood for years and later as an adult, developed a substance abuse addiction, which was followed by a cancer diagnosis. Once she was healed, my talented friend was able to take her experiences and let them flow through her artwork, creating beautiful paintings that spoke to healing, joy and moving forward. She used her pain to enlighten those who are currently suffering.

I've also known a few girlfriends who have emerged from difficult divorces with brand new versions of themselves. Some have lost weight and changed their look, others found romance again while others have gone back to school or jumped back into the workforce after being out for years raising their kids. Some have pursued careers they never thought they could do or picked up a much-loved sport or hobby again that they enjoyed when they were younger.

Once each of them healed from the pain of their divorces and transitioned into their new single status, they embraced the best of themselves and went out into the world with newfound confidence, courage and wisdom. What special gifts do you have to offer to the world? Are you creative, musically inclined, a good writer, a great cook or baker or great with kids? There are so many things you can pursue along with your day job and eventually turn your passion into a full-time gig. Just imagining it is the first step to making it happen!

Examples of being unique in the media

What we need today are more people who can be themselves and own it. It is so refreshing and the more unique the better. One of my favorite examples is singer and musician Phil Phillips, who won Fox's *American*

Idol competition in 2012. He was my favorite from the beginning, and I loved how he stayed true to himself the entire way through the competition. When the mentors were trying to get him to change up his image and look hipper or move away from his signature sound (like Dave Mathews with a little of Joe Cocker), he refused and just came out singing his songs in a creative way and being who he is.

Whether you like his music or not, he was a good example of someone who was going to play his music his way and be exactly who he is and those who got him (like me) would follow him and buy his soulful music and the others who didn't, didn't. Either way was fine by him.

Another reality show competition example and one of my favorites is *The Next Food Network Star* on the Food Network. I absolutely loved that show and one of the reasons is because they talk a lot about branding. They look for people who have a unique talent or quality to them and embrace their strengths, while minimizing their weaknesses. Where the contestants get in trouble along the way is when they veer off from what makes them special, or they change it up too many times, and confuse the judges.

The ones who usually get to the top three or those who end up winning the entire competition are the ones who stayed confident throughout, refined their message along the way so it was easy for people to understand and demonstrated their talents and abilities for the judges.

One of my favorite competitors was Melissa d'Arabian of season nine. Melissa was a home cook competing against trained chefs and was initially struggling with her confidence and feeling a little less than the other contestants. But close to the end of the competition, I remember her telling the judges when they were down to a few remaining contestants, that they should choose her as the *Next Food Network Star* because no one had her unique combination of personality, skills and passion for teaching as she did.

She worked past her fear of being the underdog throughout most of the competition and stood proudly at the end, confident in her own skin. I believe that one phrase summed up why she should win, and she eventually did.

I believe this applies to life as well. When you can zero in on your strengths, minimize your weaknesses, let your passions shine through and embrace all that you are without holding back or judging yourself then you have found your personal brand.

Why bother having a personal brand you ask? In my opinion, when you make it easy for people to understand your values and passions and maybe some of the challenges that have helped you to learn and grow, they will quickly either get you…or not. I have learned along the way that life is too short to waste time trying to get people to like me when I may not be their cup of tea, or maybe they are not mine, and that is perfectly fine.

The key is looking for your "tribe" of people who get you and you get them and that happens easier when you are more open about who you really are. How else are we going to know if we don't share our passions and values and get to know each other better? However, with that said, it is also good to get to know others who are different than you for a fresh perspective. I have seen this help me both personally and professionally.

Tell your story

Now it is your turn. What makes you unique and special? What are things you do that make your heart sing and is something you could do for free since you love it so much? Are you making room for it in your life? What compliments have you received from people in the past that resonate with you? What are personality attributes that you have viewed (or others told you) that were negative that you can minimize or turn into a positive? What are things about your background that make you different and interesting?

The world needs your uniqueness and all that you have been through makes you special and different. I run into people all the time who find out that I am a writer and say they want to write a book to tell their unique story and share it with the world. I say to them as I say to you, share your story because we all learn from each other's lessons. This book has been a blessing because it has given me a bigger audience to share some of the lessons I learned while going through a challenging time for me and my family.

When I was still in recovery mode, I saw a card in Trader Joes and the words and art by popular artist Kelly Ray Roberts jumped out at me. I kept that card at my desk hoping someday it would make even more sense than it did when I bought it. It certainly did because when I started to write this book, it became my North Star and helped me to find my authentic voice to share my story in a book. Here are the words:

Tell your story

Believe in healing

Honor your intuition

Take the journey back to yourself

Begin today

Embrace vulnerability

Do the thing you didn't think you could

Quiet the inner critic

-Kelly Rae Roberts

I encourage you to share your story with others in whatever form it takes. Maybe you could share your story in an inspiring speech at a local gathering, book, friendship circle, ministry or whenever you see someone hurting and could use a comforting word of hope from a survivor like you.

It helps us to feel more connected as a society and we can certainly use more of that, don't you think?

Writing this book has lit me up inside and been one of the most joyful soul-enriching projects I have ever worked on. Thank you for taking the time to read it and I hope you enjoyed it. Wishing you all the best as you cultivate your own special garden of life.

Blooming forward

It was several years ago when I first sat down to write the book I had dreamed of writing as I battled my way through a serious downpour in my life. During a few of my darkest days, just the thought of being able to share my lessons from a place of healing gave me hope that I would make it out ok.

The words poured out of me as I sat down to write this book in 2013, and I completed most of the writing over a two-month period. But before it was done, life challenges, full-time work and parenting two teenagers prevented me from publishing my book until now. As I look to the future, I can see that life will always have its problems and tough times. But when you do not face them alone, you can get through it, no matter what. Now when I have a difficult time – a bad week or day or simply a sad or anxious mood - I step back and allow the situation to unfold without trying to control it. I have learned to problem solve through the eyes of love, compassion and gratitude—for myself as well as for others.

*What I learned most along the way is that **to love and be loved is truly the greatest gift we can have in this imperfect life of ours**. Having positive connections with others gives us a reason to keep going after (or while still in) the downpour-- knowing people care and want us to be here.*

Also, things like being in nature, embracing laughter and fun, celebrating our uniqueness and removing shame have shown me how wonderful life can really be in both good times and bad.

I feel confident blooming forward that my life garden will continue to flourish no matter what weeds, pests or storms come my way. I wish the same for you.

With love and gratitude,

Cher (Spring 2020)

.

ACKNOWLEDGMENTS

I want to thank my sweet family who always believed in me and my idea for this book and gave me the space to write it over the summer leading up to a milestone birthday and finally publish it in 2020. I am humbled by the love you give me every single day.

Thank you to my sister, girlfriends, aunts and cousins --especially those in my small inner circle who helped me through an incredibly difficult time in my life. You always knew that during my darkest of times, I would eventually come back as my true self and see the glass half full once again.

Thank you to my parents who have generously given me love and support through the years and to my extended family and my husband's parents –I'm so thankful that you are in my life. Thank you to all the people before me who have shared their stories of happiness and surviving difficult times. By sharing, you have paved the way for others like me to share our own stories and hopefully inspire others along the way. Last but certainly not least, I want to thank God for watching over me and my family and being the ultimate loving light that led the way for me to move from a place of withering to truly flourishing!

ABOUT THE AUTHOR

CHER KNEBEL has been a professional communicator for 30 years and since 2010, also worked on the side as a social connection and happiness researcher. As a writer, speaker and founder of the blog and website, Living Happily Connected.com, Cher is passionate about sharing research, tools, tips and stories on the importance of having strong social bonds to combat loneliness and live a happier and longer life. She lives in Southern California with her husband and has two adult daughters and a cute chiweenie dog named Cooper.

www.ingramcontent.com/pod-product-compliance
Lightning Source LLC
Chambersburg PA
CBHW060943040426
42445CB00011B/981